THE
CAPTIVE
REEF

A CONCISE GUIDE TO
REEF AQUARIA IN THE HOME

TEXT, DRAWINGS AND PHOTOGRAPHS

BY

DANA RIDDLE

FOR

M.B.

ACKNOWLEDGMENTS

Terry Black
Stan Brown
Ming Chang
Noel Curry
Omer Dersom
Don Dewey
Chris Hardy
Robert Keane
Jeff Levenson
Holger Jahn
Jack Kent
John Lipsey
Jorge Medina
John Mesa
Boyce Phipps
Chris Thier
Perry Tishgart
Todd Velasco
and, of course, Donna and Ashley.

TABLE OF CONTENTS

Acknowledgments

Introduction

Part One
The Natural Environment

Part Two
The Artifical reef

Part Three
Corals

Soft Corals

Chapter	Page

INTRODUCTION

Sixty-eight million square miles of warm tropical seas cover the world's coral reefs. These often tiny creatures and their massive calcium homes have intrigued mankind for centuries. Little was known about these animals; at one time they were thought to be very industrious insects! Systematic study and classification of the coral reef and its inhabitants did not begin in earnest until the mid-nineteenth century. About this time, Sir Charles Lyell would correctly write that the reefs were the last effort of drowning continents to stay above water. Studies of the reef environment were difficult and best done on scientific cruises. A few research stations began to appear in the early 20th century. It would take a global war to stir real interests in coral studies. During World War II, conflict raged across vast tracts of the Pacific. Tiny coral islands with foreign sounding names such as Tarawa were reported as battlegrounds; a great naval battle occurred in the Coral Sea. Coral reefs slowed (and sometimes stopped) America's mighty war machine when the enemy could not. After the conflict, millions of government dollars were spent studying the biology and geology of the reefs. Tiny Pacific atolls became nuclear test sites; ironically, radioactive "tracers" would soon help scientists understand the calcification process. The environmental movement was popularized by Rachel Carson's book, "Silent Spring." Various environmental conservancies championed many causes with more than casual interest in the coral biotope. In the mid-1980's, significant numbers of corals were being imported to North America and Europe to satisy the growing demands of a growing pet industry. Environmentalists took note and successful efforts began to restrict the importation of corals.

Today, the marine aquarium hobby stands at a crossroad. If a hobbyist is willing to invest the time, effort and money in fashioning an artifical reef within the home, then he must accept the responsibility of maintaining these animals. In effect, there are thousands of amateur coral researchers around the world. There is little need to reinvent the wheel in many cases. The efforts and findings of hundreds of professionals backed by millions of dollars in grant monies is available to the hobbyist. This small book details some of these findings.

Yet the hobbyist can make significant contributions in our understanding of corals in captivity. There is little reason why a magnificent captive reef in the living room cannot double as a small research station. The requirements? An eye for detail, a small log book and a willingness to share the information. It's not difficult. But above all else, the hobby should be an enjoyable responsibility; it should offer a shelter against life's pressures. Enjoy.

PART ONE
THE NATURAL
ENVIRONMENT

Chapter 1

THE CORAL REEF

The coral reef.   A bane to the ancient mariner.   A haven to the modern adventurer.   An oasis teeming with life in an ocean desert.   A refuge for colorful fishes.   A submerged world of aggression and death.   An environment where the efforts of billions of polyps of almost microscopic proportions built structures that shame man's best engineering efforts.   The coral reef is a living contradiction; one that we must understand before we can remotely hope to maintain a small portion of it within our homes.   With this understanding, our efforts can be rewarded with a piece of living furniture - one that never fails to amaze.

This introduction will be brief.   The points made about the natural habitat will be quickly reviewed before we proceed to the "nuts and bolts" of a successful reef aquarium.

As we have just seen, no one definition adequately describes a coral reef. There are many types of reefs. Technically, a collection of animals growing upon a base of dead coral is a coral reef.   Take that same assemblage of animals and place it upon a base of basalt or a soft substrate and, technically, it is no longer a reef, but, instead, a coral community. This short review will not delve into the technicalities of coral reef classifications. Instead, we will use common names in our imaginarydive across the windward and leeward reefs of a fictitious Pacific island (See Figure 1).   With this in mind, let's begin.

Figure 1

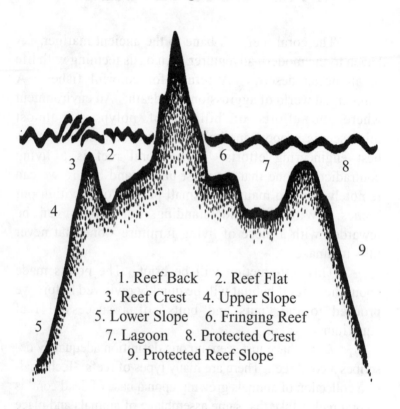

1. Reef Back   2. Reef Flat
3. Reef Crest   4. Upper Slope
5. Lower Slope   6. Fringing Reef
7. Lagoon   8. Protected Crest
9. Protected Reef Slope

The Imaginary Dive

You stand on the snow white beach of a tropical island. The day is warm and the gentle sea breezes caress your face as you look seaward. The waves breaking on the sandy beach are much smaller than those breaking over the reef crest some hundred yards in the distance. You want to swim past the breaker zone and snorkel on the seaward reef slope. As you wade into the surf, you notice the water is murky from sediment washed towards the shore. Still, the water is clear enough to see that there are no corals. As you wade into deeper water, you begin to see some bottom rubble along with an occasional live coral. This portion of the reef is called:

The Reef Back

The tide is high and suddenly you realize why there are so few corals. The reef back will be high and dry when the tide falls. Only the most hardy corals can endure this environment. Turbid water, emergence at low tide and a good amount of sedimentation just aren't conducive to good coral growth. Corals are limited to only few stubby branched Acropora and small hemispherical corals, such as Porites and Favites. Soft corals, such as the Star polyps (Clavularia) and closely-cropped Sinularia, cling to the stony rubble. The water is chest deep as you pull on your goggles and bite the snorkel's mouthpiece. The water is much clearer out here than back at the shore and, after a short swim, you can see a dramatic increaseof coral growth. You have entered the:

Outer Reef Flat

The Staghorn (Acropora) are the dominate corals here. Mostly finger-like forms of soft and stony corals grow but you also see a number of table shapes. The currents are stronger here because of the tides. It would have been a lot easier to have waited for low tide; then you could have practically walked to this point. The water's depth decreases as you glide over the underwater gardens. The coral growth thins and is replaced by beautiful pink, purple and red coralline algae. Piles of rubble litter the bottom. The waves crash nearby and, even under, water you can hear their roar. The water grows shallow as you approach the:

Reef Crest

You question your sanity in undertaking this expedition when incoming waves begin to push you back toward shore. You know that a trip at low tide would have been much more enjoyable - and wiser. Wading across this part of the reef will be possible later in the day, but you've come this far... Grasping some of the larger rubble, you hold on and, as you time the waves, you push off just as a wave passes. There's a moment of doubt as another wave tries to push you back across the crest. Then the ocean's force releases its grip, you break free and you see the:

Upper Slope

This is what you've come to see. The waves continue to tug at you as you gaze at the magnificent scene below. Large staghorn corals reach for the sun. Scores of multi-colored fishes - Tangs and Damselfishes, mostly - move gracefully with the water's motion. There is an explosion of color as they dance between the sun's rays and through the bottom's coral coverage. As the depth increases, the shape of the corals slowly changes. They appear much more fragile than those in the shallows. Water clarity is superb and it's hard to judge distance. You can see maybe 60 feet, but who knows, it might be a hundred. The reef's beauty is astonishing and you lose all sense of time. You suddenly realize it must be early afternoon, as your stomach is saying it's well past lunch time. Just one last dive before you head back in (better do it soon before the tide works against you). You take a deep breath, lower your head and kick your feet into the air, as you head down to the:

Lower Reef Slope

The water turns from teal to a dark blue as you halt your dive. There is little current and the corals are no longer branched. They're flattened or mound-like and some appear to be fleshy instead of stony. In the distance, a Barracuda slices through the water. You've never had any trouble with them before, but you broke a cardinal rule by diving by your-self. Time to head back to shore.

After lunch and a nap, you walk to the protected or lee-ward side of the island. With the wind to your back, you again gaze seaward. The sea is calm and the water laps

gently at the sand. Of course, the water will not be as still
when the tides are changing or when there is a storm, but,
overall, the ocean is at rest on this side of the island. As you
wade out chest deep, you fit the goggles to your face and
clear the snorkel. The water is cloudy, though not enough
to stop the dive, but the clarity is certainly less than on the
other side of the island. After swimming past the low tide
line, various corals begin to appear. This is a :

Fringing Reef

The staghorn corals predominate, with the growth forms
being mostly finger-like. Some table forms are also
present, as are some small massive corals, such as Porites.
Large stands of soft Leather corals (Sarcophyton) and Dead
Man's Hand corals (Sinularia) cover large patches of the
reef. The current is almost negligible and various fishes
glide effortlessly above the corals. The bottom is sandy
with some patches of mud.

Here, there are some fleshy corals living at relatively shallow depths. At a depth of about 10 feet, you see a cluster of
Elegance corals on the muddy bottom. Then you're several
hundred yards off shore and you pass the fringing reef to enter:

The Lagoon

The bottom slopes then flattens out. The sun casts glit-
tering lines across the scene. And what a scene it is! Bottlebrush and finely built Acropora corals reach up to the sun.
Mixed in between are larger table forms than you saw on the
fringing reef.   Here and there you see Goniopora and

Hydnophora corals. The nutrient level is slightly higher in the lagoon because the waves that wash over the distant sheltered reef crest will take months to displace all the lagoon's water. You notice algae including turtle grasses and Caulerpas. The water becomes shallow as you approach the:

Protected Crest

What a difference between the exposed crest and the protected crest! No fighting the currents here as the corals grow almost to the surface. You quickly discover the most difficult part is swimming across the reef crest without harming the corals with your flippers. Once past the crest, there is a sharp drop-off to the deep oceanic waters. This is the:

Protected Reef Slope

Besides the lack of current and the slight increase in water clarity, the major difference between here and the exposed reef slope on the other side of the island is the growth forms of the corals. Of course there are fragile appearing Acropora and as the depth increases, many fleshy corals appear, such as the Bubble coral (Plerogyra), Hammer corals (Euphyllia) and the Open Brain coral (Trachyphyllia).

You realize the sun is getting low and since you are quite a ways from the beach, you reluctantly turn towards the shore. The swim will be an enjoyable one though.

Chapter 2

THE MASTER MASONS

The animal that makes the coral reef possible is a relatively simple creature.   This is not to say that it is completely understood.   There are many aspects of its biology that are simply not understood at this time. This much we do know.

Corals are invertebrate animals called coelenterates (pronounced so-lent-a-rates, literally "hollow gut"). Most corals come from tropical and sub-tropical waters where the surface temperature rarely falls below 68°F for any significant time.   See Figure 2.

Corals are closely related to sea anemones and jellyfishes.   Basically, corals fall into two categories: the Alcyonarians or "soft" corals and the Zoantharians, the "stony" or "hard" corals.   The hermatypic stony corals play the most significant role of either category in reef building.   (Another group, the ahermatypic corals, do not play an important role in reef construction).   Hermatypic corals form the coral reef through their ability to deposit calcium and other elements in a relatively quick manner. A mutually beneficial relationship between the coral animal and microscopic algae imprisoned within its tissues allows this rapid skeletal growth. The algae are dinoflagellates (Genus Gymnodinium) and are commonly called zooxanthellae. Chapter 3 will detail this significant relationship.

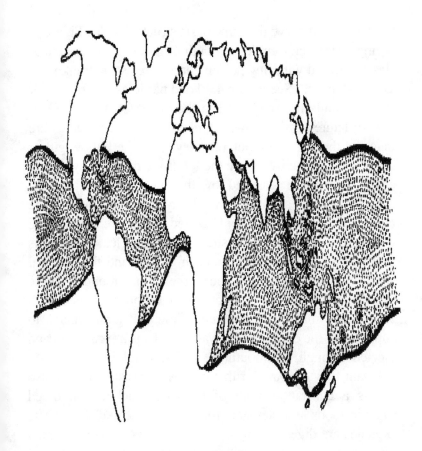

Figure 2

The shaded area indicates the geographical range of tropical soft and stony corals.

Most corals have the same basic structure.   See Figure 3. A ring of tentacles circles a mouth or mouths.   These tentacles are armed with tiny poison "darts" in a structure known as a cnidoblast. See Figure 4.   Food particles are trapped or captured and are transported to the mouth(s) by tiny whip-like structures called cilia.   Once these food particles are ingested through the mouth(s), they enter the hollow gut or gastrovascular cavity.   Here the foods are digested by gastric acids, which are secreted by the mesenterial filaments. These filaments also have the ability to extend outside the coral and capture food.   Digested foods are transported throughout the coral tissue, the mesoglea, which is sandwiched between the "stomach" lining and the external skin.   It is here that the zooxanthellae are found.   These captive algae use the products of digestion as a food with which they make carbohydrates, lipid and amino acids to supplement the coral's diet. Waste products are gathered and ejected through the mouth(s).   The coral is bathed in a constant flow of seawater that carries the waste away; it also brings a constant supply of nutrients, such as dissolved organic foods and elements for building the skeleton.   The organics are digested, the skeletal elements are concentrated and supersaturated in a thin layer of proteins, chitin or other substances.   This thin layer and mediator of calcification (more correctly, biomineralization) is called the organic matrix. When enough light, foods and "trace elements" are available, the coral will grow and deposit new skeletal material.

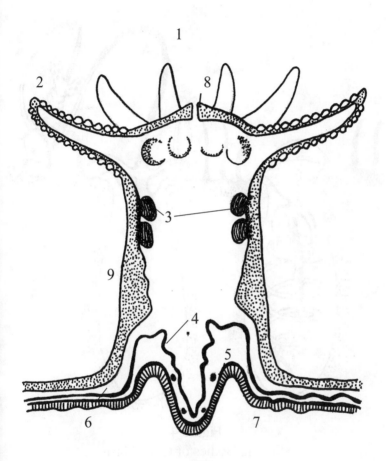

Figure 3
Anatomy of a coral polyp
1. Tentacle   2. Cnidoblasts (stinging cells)   3. Gonads
4. Mesenteries   5. Fat Bodies   6. Organic Matrix
7. Skeleton   8. Mouth   9. Mesoglea (tissue)

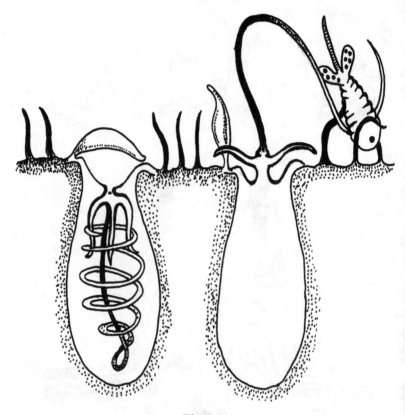

Figure 4
Stinging Bodies or Cnidoblasts
Unfired cnidoblast to the left.
On the right, a copepod has been captured and will be
transported to the mouth by the cilia.

It will also reproduce through various strategies, one of which, is sexual in nature and involves the gonads or sex organs. These are located near the mouth opening.

Many environmental factors can affect coral growth. These include:

Light
Water Movement
Oxygen
pH
Nutrition
Sedimentation
Predation
Overgrowth
Aggression
Emergence
Wave Action
Temperature

With the exception of emergence and sedimentation (which are not usually factors the aquarist must deal with), these requirements will be discussed in some detail in this work.

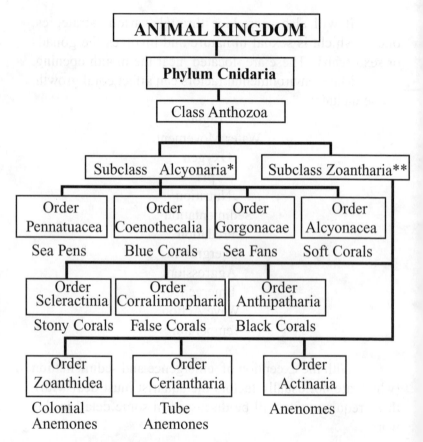

* Octocorals - Tentacles grouped in multiples of eight.
** Hexacorals - Tentacles grouped in multiples of six.

Chapter 3

CORALS, PHOTOSYNTHESIS AND ZOOXANTHELLAE

Perhaps no other subject has been scrutinized as closely as the relationship between the coral animal and its captive algae. Without this partnership, the coral reefs and communities would not exist. Zooxanthellae and their photosynthetic by-products are so important this chapter will be devoted to the subject.

Solar Radiation

Solar radiation, or light, powers every ecosystem on earth, including the coral reef. We tend to think of the equatorial regions as receiving the most amount of light. Actually, the South Pole in December gets the most, but, on average, the latitudes of 5 N to 5 S are the "sunniest." Graph 1 shows the seasonal variation of solar radiation at the equator.

If we have studied light, we know that it is composed of different wavelengths measured in nanometers (nm), which is billionths of a meter. The human eye is able to see reflected or refracted light in wavelengths of about 400nm to 700 nm. Table 1 lists the wavelengths and associated colors.

Table 1	
Color and Associated Wavelength of Visible Light	
Wavelength	Color
400 - 430	Violet
430 - 480	Blue
480 - 490	Green-Blue
490 - 510	Blue -Green
510 - 530	Green
530 - 570	Yellow-Green
570 - 580	Yellow
580 - 600	Orange
600 - 680	Red
680 - 750	Purple

Immediately below 400nm is the Ultra-Violet (UV) radiation range.   Just above 700nm is the Infrared (IR) radiation, which we perceive as heat.

Certain wavelengths are good at promoting photo-synthesis; others are not.   The portion of solar or artificial radiation that can trigger photosynthesis is known as Photo-synthetically Active Radiation (PAR).   There are meters that can measure PAR just as there are meters that can measure visible light.   Approximately 20% of visible light is PAR, which can be measured in many units. We'll use MicroEinsteins per Square Meter per Second (μE m s).

Water Clarity and PAR

Water clarity depends upon many factors.   When suspended particles scatter light and prevent it from further penetrating the water column, the water is said to be turbid.

Turbidity may be caused by varying amounts of zooplankton and phytoplankton, sediments churned up by wave or storm action or from run-off from land masses. Dissolved organic matter (gilvin) may tint the water yellow and inhibit light transmission.

Scientists have classified seawater into different categories according to its clarity. The two major groups are the blue Oceanic waters and the green Coastal waters. Both groups are divided into subgroups: there are Oceanic Types I, II, III and Coastal Types 1, 3, 5, 7, 9. Oceanic waters are clearer than Coastal Types; Type 1 or I is clearer than higher number types. Most corals come from Coastal waters. Clear waters of the Great Barrier Reef are Coastal Type 1 to 3. In many areas, waters (around leeward islands in the China Sea, for instance) are quite turbid and are Coastal Type 5. Graphs 2, 3 and 4 (at the end of this chapter) show the transmission of selected wavelengths at different depths for three types of seawater.

Photosynthesis

Photosynthesis is the production of chemical compounds by chlorophyll-containing plants when exposed to light. More specifically, it is the formation of sugars (carbohydrates) from simpler substances - carbon dioxide and water. Without sufficient light and photosynthesis, life on earth would not exist. Before proceeding, there are several terms we should be familiar with:

Respiration - Utilization of the products or by-products of photosynthesis and the energy contained within. In nature, there must be this balance:

> The Rate of Respiration will equal the Rate of Photosynthesis

Compensation Point - If light levels are just sufficient to power photosynthesis, then oxygen production will be proportional to the amount of light. When the oxygen level is enough for carbon dioxide to be produced during respiration, this is called the compensation point. The compensation point is generally considered to be about $\frac{1}{2}$ of the:

Saturation Point - When increasing the amount of light no longer raises the photosynthetic process (the amount of oxygen produced for instance), then the saturation point has been reached.

Photoinhibition - If too much light is provided, it is possible to "shut down" the photosynthetic process.

Zooxanthellae

Hermatypic (reef-building) corals and many soft corals contain single-celled algae called zooxanthellae. More specifically, zooxanthellae are dinoflagellates and are usually considered to be Gymnodinium microadriaticum.

It is thought there may be at least 4 strains or races of zooxanthellae.   The concentration of zooxanthellae within the coral's tissue can be as high as 30,000 per cubic millimeter.   These algae "infect" the coral during its planula stage and, once inside, lose their whip-like flagella and become non-motile (vegetative). See Figure 5.

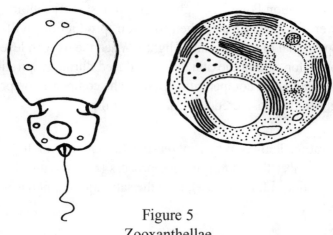

Figure 5
Zooxanthellae
Motile form, left; Vegetative form, right

The relationship between the algae and the coral is mutually agreeable: the zooxanthellae gain a protected environment and plenty of elements and compounds necessary for photosynthesis (carbon dioxide, phosphorus, nitrogen, etc.).

The coral animal, by exposing the zooxanthellae to digestive enzymes, causes the algae to become very "leaky." In this manner, the zooxanthellae provides the coral with foods or energy sources, including carbohydrates (in the form of sugars or alcohols), lipids (both saturated and unsaturated) and at least one protein precursor, the amino acid alanine. There is also good evidence that riboflavin (vitamin B_2) is also supplied. See Chapter 31 for more details about coral nutrition.

Photosynthesis and Zooxanthellae

In order for the zooxanthellae to supply its portion of nutritive substances to the coral, there must be sufficient light. If we were to measure the amount of light a coral might receive in nature, we would find lux readings of up to about 102,000 (1,900 μE m s). In order for a coral to receive this much light in an aquarium, we would have to use 10 - 175 watt metal halide bulbs! Fortunately for us reef keepers without a private electric substation in our back yards, corals do not need the full intensity of the sun and, in fact, can thrive on relatively little light. For instance, scientists have found that some corals can reach their compensation points (i.e., begin to photosynthesize) at light levels as low as 2,200 lux (41 μE m s). Of course, compensation points vary; some are as high as 10,000 lux (186 μE m s), in the case of the stony coral Favia.

NOTE: These microEinstein values apply only to sunlight. Some aquarium lights are more, some less, efficient at promoting photosynthesis.   See Chapter 8 for details about aquarium lighting.

How Corals Adjust to Light

   Corals adapt to differing light levels in many different ways.   Some methods are quite simple; the coral may expand its polyps to shade its tissues containing the zooxanthellae.   In other cases, the animal may withdraw its polyps, therefore, increasing the saturation point of the algae by "hiding" them from the light.   Other adaptations are much more complex.   Scientists have determined that exposure to low irradiance actually increases the size and number (double) of zooxanthellae.   All zooxanthellae contain Chlorophylls A and C, along with a number of other photosynthetic pigments.   Of these pigments, perhaps the most important is peridinin.   Peridinin content in the chlorophyll cells increases dramatically (up to 1.5 times) as depth increases.   Why is this important?   Because peridinins gather light outside of the range normally associated with photosynthesis.   That is, irradiance for photosynthesis is usually thought of as being in the spectral range of about   400nm to 550nm to 680nm.   Peridinin (which transfers its collected energy with almost 100% efficiency to Photosystem I) shifts the range of light energy collected to mostly 500nm to 560nm. Top end collection is still about 680.

Response to Different Colored Lights

Many experiments have been conducted on corals using different colored lights. White, blue, green and red lights have been evaluated. The colors best promoting photosynthesis are white and blue. Other experiments showed photosynthesis to increase as much as 30% under blue lighting when light fluctuations (such as those caused by passing waves) occurred.

Oxygen, the Poison

Zooxanthellae produce oxygen when sufficient light is available. Corals need oxygen, but too much of a good thing is bad, in fact, potentially toxic. Oxygen is harmful or deadly at hyperbaric (slight over pressure) pressures and animals containing symbiotic alga (corals, anemones, hydras, etc.) must deal with this pressure or perish. The "bad" form of oxygen is the radical oxygen (O^{-2}) and hydrogen peroxide (H_2O_2). Fortunately, enzymes (a form of proteins) can neutralize the danger. These enzymes, known as superoxide dimutases (SOD for short), contain microamounts of metals: there is a copper-zinc SOD, an iron SOD and a manganese SOD. Copper is believed to be the most important metal in deactivating hyperbaric oxygen. Zinc is thought to play a part in the structure of the enzyme, but can be replaced by other metals, including cobalt, mercury and cadmium.

Corals, Light and Water Movement

It is often (incorrectly) believed that light is the single determining factor that determines where a coral can live in a suitable environment.

It can't be denied that light is an important factor, but water currents play a significant part.   As depth increases, corals change shapes with some predictability. These changes seem to be more of a response to water flow rather than light.   See Figure 6.

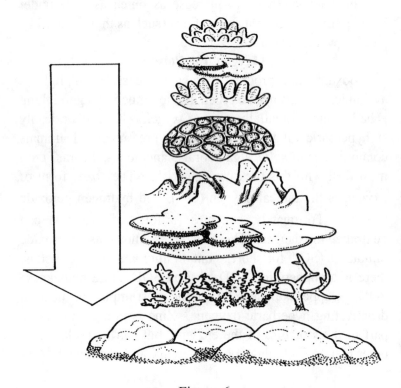

Figure 6
Water movement and amount of light affect a coral's shape.
Arrow indicates decreasing light and/or water movement.

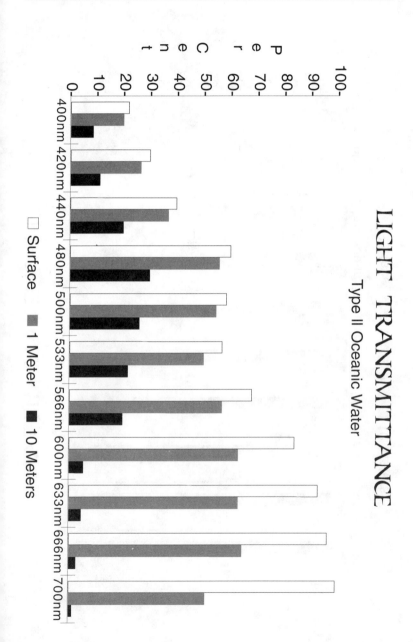

LIGHT TRANSMITTANCE

Type II Oceanic Water

□ Surface   ■ 1 Meter   ■ 10 Meters

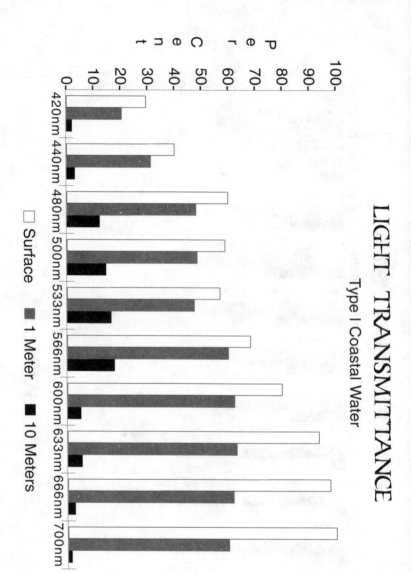

LIGHT TRANSMITTANCE

Type I Coastal Water

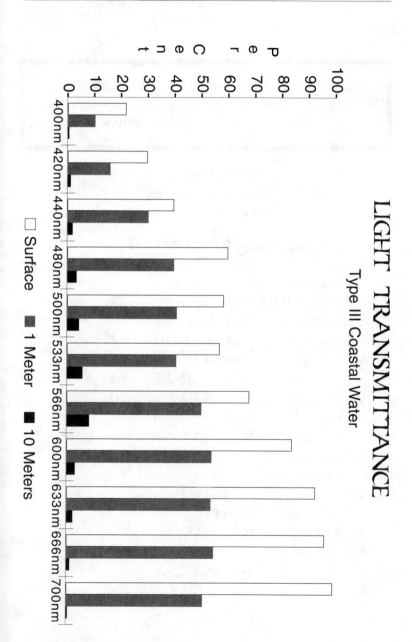

LIGHT TRANSMITTANCE
Type III Coastal Water

☐ Surface ■ 1 Meter ■ 10 Meters

Depth and Irradiance for Various Stony Corals on a
Windward Lagoon Reef Noumea Reef, New Caledonia
Irradiance in % of Surface Values

The Staghorn Corals
Family Acroporidae
Genus Acropora

Acropora digitifera, 0-0.5 meter (92%)
A. humilis, 0-0.5 meter (92%)
A. millepora, 0-0.5 meter (92%)
A.variabilis, 0-0.5 meter (92%)
A. intermedia, 0.5-3.5 meters (56 - 92%)
A. palifera, 0.5-3.5 meters (56 - 92%)
A. formosa, 0.5-3.5 meters (56 - 92%)
A. hyacinthus (table form), 0.5-3.5 meters (56 - 92%)
A. cytherea (table form), 0.5-3.5 meters (56 - 92%)
A. florida, 2-3.5 meters (56 - 85%)
A. clathrata (table form), 3.5-6 meters (43 - 56%)
A. hyacinthus, 3.5-6 meters (43 - 56%)
A. cytherea, 3.5-6 meters (43 - 56%)
A. squamosa, 6-8.5 meters (35 - 56%)
A. haimei, 6-8.5 meters (35 - 56%)
A. acculeus, 6-8.5 meters (35 - 56%)
A. subglabra, 6-8.5 meters (35 - 56%)
A. formosa, 8.5-9.5 meters (32 - 35 %)
A. palifera, 8.5-9.5 meters (32 - 35%)

The Cactus Corals
Family Agaricidae
Genus Pavona

Pavona clavus, 6-8.5 meters (35 - 43%)
P. praetorta, 6-8.5 meters (35 - 43%)

The Cup Corals
Family Dendrophyllidae
Family Turbinaria

Turbinaria peltata, 9-15 meters (22 -32%)
T. globularis, 9-15 meters (22 - 32%)

The Honeycomb and Mushroom Corals
Family Faviidae
Genus Goniastrea

Goniastrea retiformis, 0.5-2 meters (85 - 92%)

Genus Favia

Favia favus, 0.5-2 meters (85 - 92%)
F. pallida, 0.5-2 meters (85 - 92%)
F. rotumana, 0.5-2 meters (85 - 92%)
F. maxima, 8.5-9.5 meters (32 - 35%)

The Mushroom Corals
Family Fungiidae
Genus Fungia

Fungia fungites, 9-15 meters (22 - 32%)

The Finger Corals
Family Meaulinidae
Genus Hydnophora

Hydnophora microconus, 0.5-2 meters (85 - 92%)
H. exesa, 9-15 meters (22 - 32%)

The Flower Pot Corals
Family Poritidae
Genus Goniopora

Goniopora stokesi, 9-15 meters (22 - 32%)

The Open Brain Corals
Family Trachyphylliidae
Genus Trachyphyllia

Trachyphyllia geoffroyi, 15-25 meters (less than 22%)

Depth for Various Stony Corals
on a Protected Fringing Reef
Apo Reef, Mindoro, Philippines

The Staghorn Corals
Family Acroporidae
Genus Acropora

A. formosa, 0-45 meters with majority at 0-6 meters
A. spicifera (table form), 0-3 meters
A. aspera, 0-3 meters
A. exquisita, 6-35 meters
A.digitifera, 0-3 meters
A. speciosa, 6-25 meters
A. robusta, 3-6 meters
A. nastua, 3-6 meters
A. hyacinthus, 6-15 meters

The Elegance, Hammer and Bubble Corals
Family Caryophylliidae
Genus Catalaphyllia (Elegance coral)

Catalaphyllia jardinei, 3-6 meters

Genus Euphyllia (Hammer coral)
Euphyllia grabrescens, 3-15 meters

Genus Plerogyra (Bubble coral)
Plerogyra simplex, 6-15 meters
P. eurysepta, 15-25 meters

The Cup Corals
Family Dendrophyllidae
Genus Turbinaria

Turbinaria calicularis, 25-35 meters
T. glabularis, 15-25 meters
T. rugosa, 6-15 meters

The Closed Brain Corals
Family Faviidae
Genus Favia

Favia speciosa, 0-25 meters
F. laxa, 6-15 meters
F. matthai, 15-25 meters
F. valenciennesi, 6-15 meters
F. rotumana, 3-6 meters and 15-25 meters
F. amicorum, 3-6 meters
F. favus, 3-6 meters
F. pallida, 0-3 meters

F. stelligera, 6-15 meters

Family Goniastrea

Goniastrea retiformis, 0-3 meters
G. planulata, 3-15 meters
G. parvistella, 3-15 meters
G. pectinata, 3-15 meters

The Mushroom Corals
Family Fungiidae
Genus Fungia

Fungia fungites, 3-15 meters
F. echinata, 3-6 meters
F. horrida, 15-25 meters
F. samboangensis, 3-6 meters
F. scabra, 6-15 meters

The Finger Corals
Family Meaulinidae
Genus Hydnophora

Hydnophora exesa, (columnar), 3-6 meters
H. microconus, (plate), 6-15 meters
H. rigida, (branching), 3-6 meters

The Flower Pot Corals
Family Poritidae
Genus Goniopora

Goniopora tenella, 3-6 meters
G. burgosi, 3-6 meters
G. peduncalata, 6-15 meters
G. stokesi, 6-15 meters
G. undulata, 6-15 meters
G. minor, 15-25 meters

PART TWO

THE ARTIFICAL REEF

Chapter 4

THE MOTION OF THE OCEAN

Next to solar radiation, no other factor influences coral growth (in otherwise suitable locations) as water movement. Water movement depends upon winds, tides, waves and ocean currents which can vary seasonally.

The ceaseless flow of water profoundly affects the entire biocycle of the coral reefs.   Currents or wave action influence the shape or form a coral colony will take, when it feeds and possibly what it feeds upon.   Water temperature, water pressure, mechanical agitation and inundation create biological rhythms.

Tides

Tides are bulges of water produced by the gravitational pull of the sun and moon.   Spring tides occur every 14 days with a full (or new) moon and produce the highest or lowest tides. (They have nothing to do with the spring season). Neap tides occur in between the new and full moon phases and produce lower high and higher low tides.

Waves

Waves are usually wind generated.   As waves approach shore, they begin to "feel bottom" at $1/2$ its wavelength.   That is, wave crests that are 8 meters apart will begin to slow when water depth is 4 meters. As the "bottom" of the wave drags across the sea floor, the top of the wave continues at more or less original speed. As water depth decreases, wave crests become closer. A shallow water wave becomes unstable when water depth is $1/20$ of wavelength and the wave topples in a crash of water and foam.

Waves create a tremendous amount of force when breaking and few corals can take this full force. Generally, the most productive reefs are sheltered or protected from very strong wave action. Most reefs are subjected to relatively low energy waves. Corals in wave-washed areas are usually stoutly branched or small table and hemispherical forms.

Below about 12 meters (39 feet), wave action is not considered to be destructive (even during a hurricane) and corals can withstand the force of the waves.

Currents
Currents can be created by tides, waves, winds, temperature differences, etc. Of course, these variables make it difficult to make generalizations. However, the following current speeds have been listed in scientific works:

Great Barrier Reef : Tidal currents in crest grooves of up to 4 meters (13.1 feet) per second.

Surge channels: 50 to 80 centimeters (19.7 to 31.5 inches) per second for very short periods.

Lagoon currents : 2 - 45 centimeters (0.78 - 17.7 inches) per second, with 20 cm (7.9 inches) per second being average.

In another study, lagoon currents were measured at 10 to 20

centimeters (3.9 - 7.9 inches) per second.

Protected reef areas have been found to have currents of about 20 centimeters (7.9 inches) per second.

Generally, currents with velocities of about 60 centimeters (2 feet) per second are needed to keep coarse materials, such as sand and grit, in suspension. Heavy detritus falls out of suspension at velocities of about 30 centimeters (1 foot) per second.

Rip currents or jet currents: 50 to 80 centimeters (20 - 31 inches) per second.

Stagnation zones (where all suspended matter, both organic and inorganic, falls out of suspension): 2 -10 centimeters (0.78-3.9 inches) per second.

Currents of 40 to 60 centimeters (16 - 24 inches) per second are capable of moving coarse sands and granules of 1mm to 2mm (1/25th to 1/12th inch) in diameter.

Biological Importance of Water Motion

Coral metabolism may be affected by water motion.   It is believed that poor water flow creates a micro-boundary of stagnant water around a coral's surface and this stagnant area may contain insufficient amounts of carbon dioxide, oxygen, calcium (and other elements) as well as food particles.   Waste products and sediments may accumulate on or around the animal and, in effect, shelter it from light or smother it.

Researchers found that calcification might be reduced by as much as 25% in stagnant water.   Water flow of about 20 centimeters (7.9 inches) per second was sufficient to restore normal calcification rates.

Chapter 5

CHEMISTRY FOR CHICKENS

One of the great myths about salt water aquaria is that a great deal of knowledge of chemistry is required. This simply is not true. There are many hobbyists who have never checked any chemical parameter in an aquarium and have maintained beautiful tanks. This is well and good until the captive animals die for unknown reasons. The best explanation the aquarist can offer is, "something went wrong." Without background data to compare, the hobbyist guesses as to the problem, reestablishes the aquarium and hopes history does not repeat itself.   No real knowledge is gained.   The hobbyist may state, "I have ten years experience," when he really means, "I have one year's experience, ten times."

The value of monitoring water quality can not be un-derestimated.   This is not to imply that a chemistry degree is required.   Just as a dedicated amateur photographer may not fully understand the science of photography, this "handicap" should not stop him from taking beautiful photos or setting up a home dark room. The only thing the "shutter-bug" and the "reef-bug" needs is a concept of what he is attempting and enough working knowledge to manipulate various processes.

Don't be intimidated by foreign-sounding terms such as pH, nitrite, nitrate and redox.

We must remember not one person in the world has been born with a chemistry degree.   They had to acquire their skills.   With this in mind, we'll review the terms you'll need to know in order to monitor your reef aquarium.   Armed with this knowledge, you'll be able to prevent common problems and diagnose those that do occur.   Once these terms and concepts are mastered, you'll find yourself asking reasonable questions of dealers and advanced hobbyist (and at the same time, evaluate their knowledge).

Let's start with perhaps the most commonly measured parameter, pH, (pronounced as two letters "p - h") which is technically described as (take a deep breath):   "The logarithm of the reciprocal of the hydrogen ion concentration."   If, when the scarecrow got his brain, he'd spouted that sentence, everyone would have been greatly impressed, although few would have the faintest idea of the its meaning.   Relax.   Let's look at a practical definition. First, we'll need to know what an ion is.   By definition, an

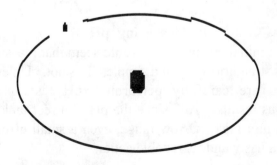

ion (eye-ahn) is an atom that carries a positive or negative electric charge due to a loss, or gain, of one or more electrons. PH is the measure of hydrogen ions and is expressed in standard pH units of 0 to 14.   When a pH measurement is below 7.0, the number of hydrogen ions is relatively high and the solution is said to be acidic.   Orange juice and battery acids, for instance, have low pH measurements.   A pH of above 7.0 is said to be basic or alkaline.   A pH of 7.0 is say to be neutral.

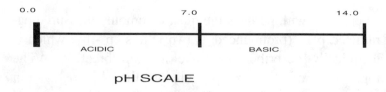

pH SCALE

Seawater and milk (and others) have basic pH readings. We want to keep the pH of the reef aquarium water at about 8.1 to 8.4, although slow fluctuations of 7.9 to 8.6 are acceptable.   HOWEVER, THE CAUSE OF THESE FLUC-TUATIONS SHOULD BE INVESTIGATED AND COR-RECTED.   See flow chart for tips on troubleshooting pH problems.

Measuring pH

Upon initial evaluation, it would seem that measurement of pH is straightforward and simple.   It is not.   Unless these analyses are carefully performed, pH tests can give erroneous results.   And since the pH of a reef tank should be kept in a fairly narrow range, even a small error might initiate a hasty and regrettable action.

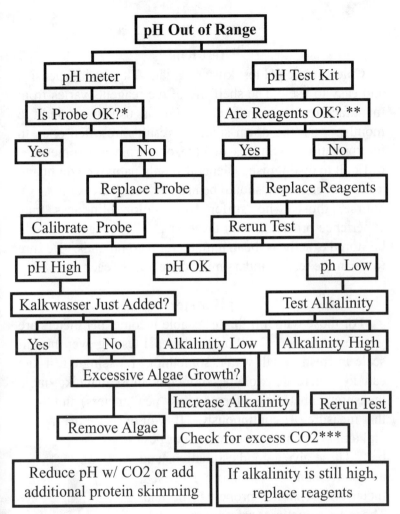

*Clean probe (follow manufacturer's recommendations). Replace probe if it fails to calibrate.
**Replace reagents if >6 mos. old or if contaminated.
***Two methods for checking excess CO2: 1.Check with a CO2 test kit. 2.Take a pH reading, aerate sample for one hour, if pH has risen, excess CO2 may exist.

Test Kits

Colorimetric pH test kits are great. They're inexpensive and easy to use. The shelf life of the reagents varies from manufacturer to manufacturer, but is usually at least 6 months. On the down side, the results are often open to interpretation. Shades of blue or purple are sometimes difficult to distinguish. Generally, only natural daylight and a white background should be used to "read" the results. Of course, those who suffer from color blindness may experience problems with these kits. The reagents should be stored exactly as the manufacturer recommends. Be sure to clean the test cylinders immediately after each use.

pH Meters

For those with a little disposable income, pH meters are wonderful tools. Good ones allow pH testing over the full scale in fresh or salt water; something few single test kits can do. There are two types of meters: those that take single measurements (often referred to as "pen" meters) and those that measure pH continuously. If you measure pH in several tanks, a pen meter may be your best bet. These give a good estimations and are convenient. For more money, a meter and separate probe can be had.  These are sometimes referred to as "laboratory grade" meters (a term that means whatever the manufacturer wants) and usually offer readings two places to the right of the decimal point (i.e., 8.29 as opposed to just 8.2).

These are not as easy to transport as the pen types. However, the lab grade meters offer continuous monitoring; this can be advantageous for observing the natural rise and fall of pH during the day, and after the addition of kalkwasser, etc. While the meter portion may last for many years, the electrode or probe should be replaced periodically. The life of a probe depends on many variables, but, generally, should last for a year to 18 months. Separate probes are fragile (I recall breaking the "bulb" end of an expensive probe a few years back).

When purchasing probes, look for those that feature: a combination electrode with an epoxy body (for durability), which should be gel-filled with at least a double junction (to maintain the flow of reference solution). The connection to the meter is usually the BNC type. Other connectors are available, but the BNC seems to be the standard for the aquarium trade.

Whichever pH meter you choose, from time to time it will have to be calibrated. For "pen" types, this will be before each use; for "lab" types, about once a month, if used for continuous monitoring. The electrode should be cleaned according to the manufacturer's directions before each calibration. Use only fresh buffers that have not passed their expiration dates (use 7.0 and 9.0 or 10.0 calibration solutions for measuring saltwater or African cichlid tanks). Discard the buffer solution used during calibration - do not reuse it. Calibrate the electrode in separate small containers used only for each individual buffer. DO NOT calibrate the probe in the large bottle of buffer. DO NOT pour the pH buffers into the aquarium to adjust the pH! Your captive fishes and corals will hate you forever.

Carbonate Hardness or Alkalinity

Alkalinity (or carbonate hardness) and pH are closely related, but are not the same thing. Alkalinity is the measure-

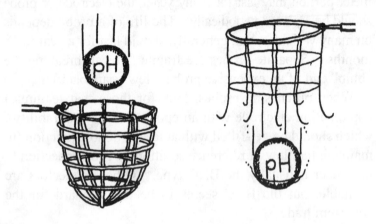

ment of the water's ability to neutralize acids. The substances most often used to "destroy" acids are carbonates, bicarbonates, hydroxides and borates (phosphorus and silicates also buffer against acidity, but their presence in the marine aquarium is less than desirable, so they will not be discussed here). Strong alkalinity will prevent small amounts of acids from causing a drop in pH. A weak alkalinity will not stop a drop in pH from the same amount of acid. Think of alkalinity as a safety net for pH. Alkalinity is usually expressed as German Carbonate Hardness (DKH), as milliequivalents per liter (meq/l), or as calcium carbonate ($CaCO_3$) in parts per million (ppm) or milligrams per liter (mg/l), which, for our purposes, is the same thing as ppm.

Conversion Factors for Alkalinity
2.8° German Carbonate Hardness = 1 milliequivalent per
liter = 50 ppm CaCO3

This test can be performed in several different ways. For the range we would normally expect to find alkalinity in a marine aquarium, the best way is to add an acid to a sample of aquarium water until the pH drops to 4.5. Precise alkalinity measurements are performed with a pH meter and an acid of known strength, or normality. However, good results can be obtained by using an alkalinity test kit. These use an acid of known strength and a chemical reagent (pronounced ree-agent) that changes color at a pH of about 4.5.

The natural alkalinity of seawater is usually about 7 or 8 DKH. Opinions vary on the best alkalinity for the marine aquarium. While maintaining natural levels is certainly recommended, some research conducted in the 1960's suggest high alkalinity levels encourage calcification, even if inhibiting phosphorus is present. This would be a good experimental project for an advanced hobbyist.

Calcium

Calcium is an important element in seawater. It is used by many plants and animals for skeleton formation. It can also be used as an alkalinity source. The calcium concentration varies through the world's oceans. The average concentration is generally agreed to be about 400 milligrams per liter (mg/l), or ppm.

In the aquarium, calcium levels should be maintained at slghtly higher concentrations because most test kits can't distinquish between calcium and certain other elements. Therefore, maintaining a level of 500 mg/l will ensure that enough calcium is available. Calcium is often added in the form of kalkwasser (German for lime water.) Kalkwasser is normally calcium oxide (CaO) or calcium hydroxide (CaOH).

Detractors often oppose this form of calcium, as it is not a particularly rich source of calcium and has a high pH. It is up to the aquarist to evaluate the usefulness of this calcium form and its high pH, but there are two points not generally discussed about kalkwasser. It is possible for kalkwasser to combine with phosphorus and fall out of solution (known as precipitation). This is known to occur at a pH of about 10. Certainly, this is a useful water pretreatment method. It also occurs to a limited extent when kalkwasser is added to a filter sump. Locally, the pH will rise and the phosphorus will fall out of solution as a yellow-brown precipitate. At slightly higher pH (about 11), nitrates can also be indirectly removed. It seems that dissolved ammonia (NH3, or ammonium, NH4) cannot stay in solution at a high pH and will "flash" off from the water as a gas. Again, lime treatment of makeup water is beneficial if ammonia is present. Ammonia removal also occurs on a limited basis when kalkwasser is added to the filter sump.

Ammonia, other nitrogenous compounds and phosphorus, will be discussed in more detail later in this chapter.

Strontium

Strontium is an alkaline earth metallic element found in natural seawater at a concentration of about 8 milligrams per liter (mg/l).   It is found to be concentrated in many coral skeletons and often makes up 1% of the skeletal weight. There is some debate about strontium being an essential element for skeletal growth though, there is at least one scientific journal reference that states corals grow faster when strontium concentrations increase.

Strontium supplements are readily available to the hobbyist.   Test kits for strontium exist.

Salinity

Perhaps the most outstanding feature of the oceans, besides their size, is the fact that they are salty.   Every aquarist knows the saltiness of the water must be accurately gauged. We can learn from scientific literature but there is a problem.   Scientists almost always express the "saltiness" in terms of salinity.   Salinity is the concentration of dissolved elements in water.   It is expressed as grams of dissolved material per kilogram of water (g/kg), which is parts per thousand (0/00).   Salinity is remarkably consistent throughout the Atlantic and Pacific surface waters and varies by only 2.5 parts per thousand.   See Table 2.

Of course, the salinity of seawater trapped in a tidal pool might increase dramatically due to evaporation; conversely, tropical monsoons can drastically reduce the salinity of a reef flat at low tide.

Table 2		
Salinities of the Atlantic and Pacific Oceans at Various Latitudes		
Latitude		Atlantic
Pacific		
20 N	36.47	n/a
15 N	35.92	34.67
10 N	35.62	34.29
5 N	34.98	34.29
Equator	35.67	34.85
5 S	35.77	35.11
10 S	36.45	35.38
15 S	36.79	35.57
20 S	36.54	35.70
25 S	n/a	35.62

As a reference, likely collection point latitudes are listed:

Indonesian islands - 8°S Marshall Islands - 10°N
Fiji - 18°S   Philippines - 10°N
China Sea - 9°N   Coral Sea - 20°S
Caribbean islands - 18°N

Converting Salinity to Density or Specific Gravity
Salinity can be measured with a hydrometer. The use and proper reading of this instrument is covered in hobbyist literature and will not be reviewed.

Hydrometers made for the aquarium trade offer only acceptable accuracy. Density is dependent on temperature and, without knowing what temperature the hydrometer is calibrated, they offer only an approximation of true specific gravity. A quality hydrometer will be calibrated to National Bureau of Standards for salt solutions at 15° C (59° F). "Aren't these just for researchers?" you may ask. Well, scientists do use them. But isn't every reef keeper actually a researcher? You bet they are.

A "lab grade" hydrometer may be twice the price of a "hobbyist grade" instrument. However, by knowing the calibration temperature and using simple conversion tables, the hobbyist can accurately measure specific gravity at any reasonable temperature. See Tables 3 and 4.

Table 3	
Salinity to Density Conversion Table	
34.2 = 1.0254	35.7 = 1.0265
34.4 = 1.0255	35.6 = 1.0266
34.5 = 1.0256	35.9 = 1.0267
34.6 = 1.0257	36.0 = 1.0268
34.8 = 1.0258	36.2 = 1.0269
34.9 = 1.0259	36.3 = 1.0270
35.0 = 1.0260	36.4 = 1.0271
35.1 = 1.0261	36.6 = 1.0272
35.2 = 1.0262	36.7 = 1.0273
35.4 = 1.0263	36.8 = 1.0274
35.5 = 1.0266	37.0 = 1.0275

Table 4
Salinity Conversions for Hydrometer Calibrated at 15° C

Salinity	Hydrometer Says:	Correct reading at:		
		22°	24.5°	27°
24.6	1.018	1.0195	1.0201	1.0208
27.2	1.020	1.0215	1.0222	1.0229
29.8	1.022	1.0235	1.0242	1.0249
32.4	1.024	1.0256	1.0262	1.0270
35.0	1.026	1.0276	1.0283	1.0290
37.6	1.028	1.0296	1.0303	1.0311

Temperature

Before discussing temperature, let's get the conversion factors out of the way. If you're not familiar with these, learn them or at least practice with them so you get a good idea of how certain C readings relate to F readings.

Table 5
Temperature Conversion Formulas
To convert C to F .... (C X 1.8) + 32 = F
To convert F to C .... (F - 32) ÷ 1.8 = C

Temperature plays a very important role in coral reef biology. Corals are most successful in suitable shallow seas where the water surface temperature does not fall below 18° C for any significant length of time.

Temperature affects many important parameters. It affects salinity and the amount of dissolved gases the water can hold; dissolved oxygen (DO) is generally higher when temperature is lower and all other conditions are the same. Biological activity is usually higher at warmer temperatures. (Bacterial activity will double for every 10° C rise in temperature between 0 and about 35° C.) Researchers routinely report water surrounding coral reefs to be 32° C.

Temperature in the Reef Aquarium

If we want to mimic the conditions of a natural reef within our aquarium, then it is OK to let the temperature get as high as 32° C, right? Wrong, maybe dead wrong. The aquarium is not the ocean; it is its own unique microcosm. Since bacteria are much more active at higher temperatures and the DO level in an aquarium is likely to be lower (due to oxygen solubility at elevated temperature and the oxygen demand of the bacteria and other tank inhabitants), there is little margin for error. Should an animal die or a major piece of equipment fail (such as a circulation pump or protein skimmer), oxygen levels could drop rapidly. Of course, the same would happen at a lower temperature but at a relatively slower rate.

Corals act quite markedly to temperature and some species have been found to favor rather narrow temperature ranges. For instance, maximum growth rates were observed in the stony corals Porites and Pocillopora at 26° to 27° C; growth dropped off rapidly with a rise or fall outside the optimal range. Stony corals Montipora, Pavona and Cyphastrea favor temps of 24° to 25° C. The upper end of the water in the former case is rather warm; it would seem temperature control isn't really necessary. Haven't marine biologists told us that corals survive in 32° C (90° F) water? Yes, but that is not true for all species, especially those from deeper water.

Corals react to stress in different manners. A typical stress-induced reaction is the release of large amounts of mucus. Elevated temperatures can cause this. The mucus enters the aquarium food chain and is dinner for millions of bacteria. Exactly what we do not need when the bacterial action is already high and DO is marginal. When a sublethal temperature of approximately 33° C is reached, many corals will expel their symbiotic algae, zooxanthellae. At about 34° to 35° C, most corals will die.

Another interesting point should be made about temperature. This concerns the coral's uptake of iodine, which is reportedly used to detoxify hyperbaric oxygen within the coral's tissue. Iodine uptake is linear up to about 25° C and doubles between 25° and 30° C. At 32° C, iodine uptake stops and the coral may die of oxygen poisoning.

At the opposite end of the scale, low temperatures can also be injurious or fatal. At 16° to 20° C, corals lose their zooxanthel-lae, a condition called bleaching. At 15° C, corals will die within a few days from undetermined causes.

Measuring Temperature

Temperature measurements are obviously important. Yet we often risk an investment of hundreds or even thousands of dollars on a cheap thermometer that may be in error by about 3° C (5 F).

It would be cheap insurance indeed to invest $25 or so in a certified thermometer. ASTM or NIST thermometers are available. Good thermometers will be mercury-filled, have etched markings and respond rapidly to temperature changes. My favorite thermometer is an ASTM Saybolt Viscosity, #17F.

Redox Potential

Short for Reduction-Oxidation Potential (and pronounced ree-dox, not red-ox), this term has been used often in recent aquaria literature. It may also be referred to as ORP, or Oxidation-Reduction Potential. It is an important water quality yardstick. There is a terrific amount of science behind this parameter, but worry not, the aquarist must only understand a few things. First, redox is measured in millivolts, which is abbreviated as mV. Millivolt readings of 1 to 1000 indicates an aerobic (with oxygen) condition. Less than zero (negative mV) indicates anaerobic conditions, that is, conditions without molecular oxygen. Is it really necessary to monitor redox? Absolutely not. But it is useful in certain instances. Falling redox values can indicate a death in an aquarium and the aquarist can take action before the decay process gets serious. Monitoring mV trends in a heavily stocked or well-fed aquarium can monitor the efficiency of the filter system or protein skimmer. Redox should be compared against pH, since redox falls when pH rises and vice versa. Since redox is almost always discussed with ozone, that will be our next topic.

Ozone

Ozone is strange stuff. In the summer, when ozone and smog combine around heavily populated areas, its presence is often reported as a warning to those with respiratory problems. Yet we need it high up in the atmosphere to plug holes that let the harmful radiation through. If some scientist can figure out that trick...

What is ozone? We know molecular oxygen is usually two joined oxygen molecules, O_2. Ozone is three oxygen atoms, O_3, and it is oxygen with an attitude. It is aggressive; it wants to rid itself of the extra oxygen molecule. When it does, it oxidizes, it burns and it doesn't care if it's the nasty organic stuff in your aquarium water or the tissues in your nose. If properly controlled it is perfectly safe; in fact, ozone is routinely injected into swimming pools to maintain superb health conditions and clarity. Ozone can be a bonus to an aquarium, but should really be used in combination with a redox controller. A controller is a little different than a redox monitor. The controller will have at least one "set point" to tell the ozone generator when to operate and when to stop.

Ozone can be produced by exposing air or oxygen to UV light or by passing it through an electrical arc.

Redox in the Marine Aquarium

It is difficult to recommend an ORP level for the reef tank. Only your animals know for sure. The Staghorn coral (Acropora) may enjoy a redox of, say, 400 mV, while the Elegance coral (Catalaphyllia) is found in sedimentary oozes with its skeleton buried in anaerobic muck.

Redox values change in the oceans with the tides. The careful and observant aquarist may want to experiment with differing redox levels and its effect on various corals. Generally, redox values of 200mV to 450mV for community reef tanks seems to be sufficient. The hobbyist however should carefully observe the captive animals when adjustments are made to the redox value then base the apparent benefit to the aquarium on the appearance of the animals and not just on some number.

Nitrogen Compounds

Nitrogen compounds are quite common in reef tanks. They are a necessary evil. They must be present in micro amounts, not in high quantities. Some forms are deadly to tank inhabitants. Others are merely nuisances. Fortunately for us, nature has a marvelous system for dealing with nitrogen called the:

Nitrogen Cycle

Your child just can't stand to see the fishes in your reef tank go hungry. So, every afternoon you let him feed them a small amount of food. The fish are reasonably happy, your son is happy, but you are miserable. The nitrate level in your aquarium is sky high. Why? Some one (guess who) has failed to provide the proper conditions within the aquarium for the nitrogen cycle to function as it should.

Let's examine what happens when the fish were fed and what went wrong. Then we'll examine ways to correct the situation.

The fish food you've added to the aquarium contains pro-teins. That's great because fish need them; so do corals and other living things. Proteins are composed of amino acids, which are about 15% nitrogen. Now the fish eats most of the food and incorporates some of the proteins into its own tissue as it grows. What it doesn't use is expelled as partially digested protein or as ammonia (which is the nitrogen (N) combined with 3 or 4 hydrogen atoms to become ammonia or ammonium, respectively). No problem, except ammonia or ammonium is toxic. Nature comes to our rescue as there are bacteria (such as Nitrosomonas species) that "eat" ammonia ($NH3$ or $NH4$) and strip away the hydrogen atoms and replace them with two oxygen atoms, which makes $NO2$ or nitrite. Big problem - nitrite is toxic! Another form of bacteria (Nitrobacter) eats the nitrite and adds a third oxygen mole-cule to the $NO2$ to make $NO3$, which is called nitrate. As we can see, the conversion of ammonia to nitrite and then nitrate requires a good deal of oxygen. The equations look like this:

$$NH3 + 1.5 \ O2 + Nitrosomonas = NO2 + H+ \ and \ H2O$$

(notice that one hydrogen ion is produced, which will deplete alkalinity and may lower pH) =

$$NO2 + 0.5 \ O2 = NO3$$

Unlike ammonia, ammonium and nitrite, nitrate is not really toxic. But it can cause problems and, by law, drinking water should not contain more than 10 ppm of nitrate. Since you shouldn't drink water with 10 ppm nitrate, why would you want your fishes and corals living in that much or more? You don't. So, how do you get rid of it?

You could get the nitrate level to nothing (eventually) by not feeding the tank but, of course, the fishes and corals will die. Not an option. Acceptable methods include denitrification filters, nitrate removing compounds, algae filters, protein skimming, etc. Fortunately, the best method is, over the long run, also the cheapest. Pay attention, things like this occur only several times in a lifetime.

There are bacteria that love to use nitrate for their own selfish reasons, but they need a proper home in which to live. By failing to provide proper housing for these little guys, the aquarist has brought the high nitrate levels upon himself. Where is this housing? Very simple. It is deep with the pores of good quality live rock or in the anoxic zones of aquarium sand. Within these pores or sand layers, bacteria live without molecular oxygen.

But they still need oxygen in order to live. So, where do they get it? Remember nitrate, NO_3? There's a great source. These bacteria strip away the oxygen molecules to breathe and leave one nitrogen atom, which bubbles out of the tank as nitrogen gas. This process is called denitrification. The equation appears so:

$$2\ NO_3 + 3H+ \text{ and an Organic substance} = N_2 + 3HCO$$

A couple of notes about denitrification. Notice that nitrogen gas and bicarbonate are the end products. One half of the alkalinity destroyed during nitrification is returned by denitrification. The organic (carbon) source is usually available naturally in aquarium water. Waters containing high amounts of nitrate may require an added source of carbon; methanol is generally used, although many other substances can be used. (I once told a clerk at a liquor store I was going to add the vodka I had just purchased to an aquarium. I'll always remember his strange look.)

We can easily see the bacteria are eager to do the job if we just give them a chance. In many aquariums, especially those that are heavily fed, it will not be possible to add enough rock or sand to provide enough housing for the nitrate-eating "bugs." So, what do you do? Reduce the amount of nitrogen added to the tank. We've already said less feeding may not be a possibility; so, we install a protein skimmer to remove the nitrogen containing compounds. If a protein skimmer is in place, consider a second or larger, more efficient unit. If the tank isn't overfed and good skimming with plenty of rock and sand is used and nitrates are still high then consider a denitrification filter or nitrogen-removing compounds. Of course the make-up water should be checked for nitrates and controlled if found to be present. Limiting nitrogen compounds will ease algae growth in the aquarium, but limiting our next subject of discussion is a more efficient means.

Phosphorus

Phosphorus is an element (P). It is in every living cell a an energy source. Since it is in cells, obviously it is in our foods as well as fish and invert foods. Everything needs phosphorus for growth - everything including those forms of undesirable reef tank occupants, such as the nuisance algae commonly referred to as "micro-algae." Phosphorus control in the aquarium is not a concern if micro-algae is not a problem an the tank doesn't contain corals. In most reef tanks, however phosphorus is a concern because elevated levels inhibit the calcification process. Of course, the algae will grow over the non-growing corals and the whole scene will be a "beautiful one of filamentous algae gently waving in the water current.

Controlling Phosphorus

First and foremost, don't overfeed the tank. Don't starve the animals either; find that happy medium and stick to it. Monitor phosphorus levels with a high quality test kit. Make sure the kit is made for use for saltwater samples. All test kits currently marketed in the pet industry measure only a form of phosphorus called orthophosphate. These kits estimated only a portion (but usually the major portion) of phosphorus compounds in the water. Therefore, algae may be growing wildly while the test kit shows "zero" orthophosphate. What is needed is a Total Phosphate test kit for saltwater. When one is eventually marketed, it will most likely use the Persulfate method of phosphorus detection.
For full details on controlling nuisance algae, see Chapter 6.

Oxygen

Oxygen (O^2) is important to every living thing. Even in anaerobic processes where dissolved oxygen (DO) is not available, atomic oxygen must be present for the anaerobes to survive.

Dissolved oxygen should be found in concentrations of at least 2 mg/l (or parts per million -ppm, if you prefer) for bacteria and other creatures (including most reef aquaria inhabitants) to function properly. Often, saltwater tanks using only subsand filters will have DO levels of around 4 ppm. Properly maintained reef aquaria with trickle filters (good) or large protein skimmers (best) will have DO levels approaching the saturation point; that is, for a given temperature salinity and pressure, the water is holding as much oxygen as normally possible. It is possible to supersaturate saltwater with DO, but this takes extraordinary means to do so. In nature, the violent aeration of a wave-hammered reef crest may have dissolved oxygen levels exceeding 18 ppm, while the saturation point is close to 7 ppm. Deeper water below the reef crest may have saturated DO until around 9 meters (30 feet).

Do fishes and corals need high DO? Apparently fishes are not adversely affected by abnormally high DO and can swim through oxygen gradients with ease. Corals probably do not need lots of oxygen during the day as their zooxanthellae saturate the coral's tissues with the element. The coral must then detoxify the hyperbaric oxygen or risk death. The coral however will need a good oxygen supply during the evening.

Being able to maintain O^2 at or near the saturation point in the aquarium indicates that all biochemical, physical and chemical oxygen demands have been satisfied and an oxygen "buffer" exists to hedge against sudden drops.

What Is the Oxygen Saturation Point?

Whole books have been written on this subject and these contain pages of mathematical formulae. For our purposes, we'll disregard barometric pressures and other parameters that only moderately affect the DO content of salt water.   We will consider temperature, salinity and altitude.   Table 6 lists these estimations.

Table 6
Dissolved Oxygen Levels at Various Temperatures
and Salinities

Temp. °C	Salinity, PPT				
	0	30	32	34	36
21	9.0	7.5	7.4	7.3	7.2
22	8.8	7.4	7.2	7.1	7.1
23	8.7	7.2	7.1	7.0	6.9
24	8.5	7.1	7.1	6.9	6.8
25	8.4	7.0	6.9	6.8	6.7
26	8.2	6.8	6.7	6.7	6.6
27	8.1	6.8	6.7	6.6	6.5
28	7.9	6.6	6.5	6.4	6.3
29	7.8	6.5	6.4	6.3	6.2
30	7.7	6.4	6.3	6.2	6.1

Correction Factors for Selected Cities

Altitude plays an important part in determining the oxygen saturation point in seawater.

After finding the DO level for the temperature and salinity from the above chart, use the appropriate factor to determine the estimated saturation point.

Table 7		
Dissolved Oxygen Altitude Correction Factors for Selected North American Cities		
City	Average Altitude	Correction Factor
Atlanta, GA	1,050	0.96
Baltimore, MD	20	1.00
Boston, MA	21	1.00
Chicago, ILL	595	0.98
Dallas/Ft. Worth, TX	435	0.98
Denver, CO	5,280	0.82
Detroit, MI	585	0.98
Houston, TX	40	1.00
Los Angeles, CA	340	0.99
New York, NY	55	1.00
Ottawa, Ontario	276	0.99
Philadelphia, PA	100	1.00
Pittsburgh, PA	745	0.97
Quebec, Quebec	347	0.98
Saint Louis, MO	455	0.98
San Francisco, CA	65	1.00
Toronto, Ontario	356	0.98
Washington, DC	25	1.00

For instance, a reef aquarium at sea level could contain 6.9 ppm O^2 at 34 ppt at 24° C. If the aquarium was in Denver, CO, the correction factor of 0.82 could be used, hence:

6.9 ppm Oxygen X 0.82 = 5.66 ppm

Measuring Dissolved Oxygen in the Aquarium

Several different methods can be used to determine DO. The most accurate methods involve a DO meter and polaro-graphic probe (which measures oxygen diffusion rates across a membrane) and a chemical titration method (which is usually the Winkler or modified Winkler method). Both offer results acceptable to the U.S. Environmental Protection Agency. An industrial quality DO meter is about $1,000 and up; hobbyist grade meters are much less. Both offer ease and convenience for DO measurements.

The Winkler method is a multi-step chemical test that of-fers outstanding results when properly performed. Winkler titrations are often used to calibrate DO meters. These DO test kits are reasonably priced.

A third method exists for DO determinations. It involves a glass ampule that contains a small amount of chemical sealed in a vacuum. When the ampule is broken open underwater it fills with a proper amount of water and mixes with a reagent. A chemical reaction causes the mixture to change color; the color is proportional to the amount of DO.

The ampule color is compared to a color chart and a DO estimation is made.

Chapter 6

ALGAE CONTROL

We often see photographs of a natural reef and there's not a strand of green algae in sight. It is, therefore, very easy to make the assumption that algae doesn't grow on the reefs. And that assumption would be nonsense. Reef areas will quickly grow algae if plant-eating animals are excluded. Typical lagoon algae include various Caulerpas, Turtle grass (Thalassia), Mermaid's Wine Glass (Acetabularia), etc. Reef flats have Sargassum zones. Even the exposed reef slope is called home by Halimeda and coralline red algae, including Lithophyllum, Hydrolithum and Sporolithon. Algae growth is natural and should be encouraged. But we must be very selective in the algae we allow to grow. Without due care, the aquarium will be overgrown by so-called micro-algae and the aquarist will wage a constant battle against it.

Micro-Algae in the Aquarium

A few years ago, a marine aquarium full of green filamentous algae was considered healthy. Green carpets of Derbesia and Enteromorpha covered the coral decoration. But that was OK; the algae's presence indicated that the nitrogen cycle was producing nitrates. Since the water was "conditioned," fishes more delicate than the "starter" damsels could be added. Then came the reef tank. The once desirable alga were choking the corals, often killing them. Nutrient control became a priority and the industry responded with nutrient removers, algicides and an array of natural algae "enemies."

Algae Control

Before the first drop of water is added to the reef aquarium, the hobbyist should make algae control a top priority. The live rock should be "cured," that is, the algae and animals that cannot survive in the reef aquarium should be removed either by scrubbing or by allowing the rock to remain in a separate container with no light and very good water circulation.   The rock should also be of good quality, meaning that it is porous and preferably covered with the purple, pink or red coralline algae.   (It is often said that microalgae will not grow on top of coralline algae and that is true; but it sure will grow in any pore or crack in the coralline coverage).   Most of the live rock should be fairly flat pieces with a few round ones. Using the round pieces as a base, the flat pieces should be terraced towards the back of the tank, with about 2 inches between the back rock and the aquarium glass.   Room should be allowed for a small water pump or powerhead about every two feet of tank length. The pump discharge can be pointed in the desired direction to maintain good water flow around and especially under the rock.   In this manner, detritus containing the compounds needed for algae growth will be swept towards the front of the aquarium where it can be either siphoned or, preferably, vacuumed out of the tank.

Nutrient Control

Every element needed for algae control is in good supply in the reef aquarium. Algae needs nutrients and micro-nutrients in order to survive. The macro-nutrients are carbon, nitrogen, phosphorus and potassium. The Phosphorus/Nitrogen/Carbon ratios in plant tissue is 1:7:40. It is easy to see that phosphorus is the least of the macro-nutrients and if we were to limit the supply of phosphorus, we can limit algae growth. Research has shown that 1 gram of phosphorus can give rise to 140 grams of dry algae tissue. So, we can limit the amount of dissolved phosphorus, but still have an algae problem due to the phosphorus bound in the detritus. By vacuuming the detritus out of the aquarium, we remove a major source of food for the nuisance algae. Of course, the de-

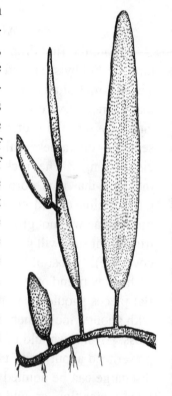

sirable forms need phosphorus too. Depending upon your tastes, desirable forms include different Caulerpas, Halimeda, Acetabularia, etc. (see Drawings). If these algae are not to your liking, another alternative is to use the high quality coralline algae rock and let the nuisance algae grow. Use the Chestnut Turban ("Turbo") snails, Astrea snails, Trochus snails, Tri-color hermit crabs, Urchin crabs or Tangs (See Drawings) to graze the algae. Use Sea Cucumbers for substrate algae control if your aquarium contains sand. These herbivores should be added to the aquarium after the live rock and as soon as the danger of ammonia spikes has passed.

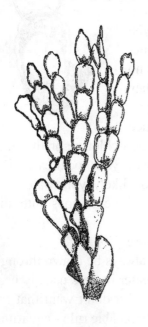

Pretreating Your Water If the water's good enough to drink, its good enough for the aquarium, right? Maybe, maybe not - no definitive answer here. Public drinking water utilities are required by law to meet some pretty tough standards and they must test the water as it leaves their treatment plant. They're also responsible for what their clean water picks up as it passes through the old plumbing in your house. It seems that old galvanized and new copper lines may add heavy metals to the water. Water companies are especially concerned about these, so to protect you from your old plumbing they add phosphorus. And it really works. It's cheap. It's harmless. And it makes algae grow like mad. What to do?

Evaluating Your Water

If you buy drinking water from a public utility, call them and find out about your water. They may tell you that it's just right for your reef tank; that it has calcium, strontium and no phosphorus or heavy metals. Or they may tell you that a flocculating agent such as ferrous or ferric iron is added  along with phosphorus. All will add chlorine or fluorine. If you are on well water, check with your local extension service. They can guide you. Most likely, your water will need some sort of pretreatment before it goes into the aquarium.

A Special Note

Water for the aquarium should always be drawn through the cold water supply line. Hot water heaters usually heat and then store water for a while. You don't want that for many reasons. Just make it an unbreakable rule - aquarium water should always come from the cold water faucet. Let the water run for at least 30 seconds to clear the water that has been standing in the house's water lines.

Pretreating for Chlorine

Chlorine is probably the most common additive to drinking water. It kills bacteria. That's good. It can also kill fish and corals. Not too good. The best way to remove chlorine is by aerating the water for a few hours. Chlorine may have combined with some nitrogen compounds in the water to form chloramines. These can be conveniently removed by chloramine removers sold in pet shops.

Pretreating for Phosphorus, Ammonia and Heavy Metals

All these can be removed from the make-up water rather

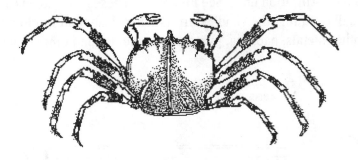

quickly and with a minimum of expense. All it takes is a heavy duty plastic bucket and a small bag of kitchen pickling lime or garden hydrated lime. It's a very good idea to wear some rubber kitchen gloves and safety glasses since we'll be dealing with some pretty caustic stuff.

To cold water in the bucket, add lime until the pH is over 10. (About half a cup of lime to 5 gallons of water as a very general guideline - check the pH). The water will get warm, maybe very warm, as a chemical reaction occurs between the water and lime. Most of the phosphorus and some metals will fall out of solution (precipitate), any ammonia will degas to the atmosphere. Allow the lime to settle in the container for a few hours and there you have it.

The water is very low in phosphorus, ammonia and metals while being full of calcium, magnesium and other elements that corals use to make their skeletons.

What To Do If Your Water Stinks

If your water smells like sulphur or leaves rusty deposits in the sink, that's a pretty good indicator that you need some heavy duty water treatment. Probably the best bet for water like this is a Reverse Osmosis (R.O.) Unit, or more correctly, a nano-filtration unit. See Figure 21. These neat gadgets actually "strain" the "bad" stuff (such as lead, chromium and other metals, bacteria, pyrogens, pesticides and other organ-

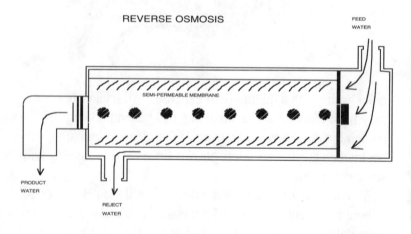

ics with molecular weights over 200) out of the water. They also strain out "good" stuff as well (such as calcium, carbonates and others), but that's the price you pay. R.O. units sometimes have prefilters for sediments and chlorine as well. The R.O. membrane, which usually looks like an almost empty roll of paper towels, is porous to small molecules, such as clean water, while it "rejects" the bad stuff in a flow of reject water. Reverse Osmosis Units waste a lot of water. Usually, 20% of the water delivered to an R.O. is actually purified. This purified water is called "product" water. Therefore, for every gallon of product water, there will be 4 gallons of "reject" water. Many factors affect the amount of product water produced. Obviously, water with high amounts of dissolved substances will produce more reject water. Cold water also produces less product water; however, water temperature of about 110 degrees F will destroy the membrane. Water from the hot water line should not be used since it may contain relatively high amounts of copper and lead. Water pressure also affects the amount of clean water produced. Most R.O. units need about 45 psi to operate; pressure ratings on the plastic housings are usually about 100 psi and should not be exceeded.

  The membrane needs to be replaced regularly, as do the sediment and carbon filters (if so equipped). They are expensive to maintain, but can still produce "good" water more economically than "distilled" water can be purchased. And, while on the note of distilled water, groceries sell it by the gallon, but there is no guarantee that it is any better than tap water. Back to R.O.; if you're interested in purchasing one, be aware that there are different types of membranes available.   Thin Film Composite (TFC) membranes are good for any applications; Cellulose Triacetate (CTA) membranes are for chlorinated waters. Both are effective in removing contaminates with one notable exception: the TFC membrane removes more nitrate than the CTA units.

Properly operated and maintained, R.O. units will remove these substances: aluminum, ammonia/ammonium, arsenic, bacteria, barium, bicarbonate, borate, boron, bromine, calcium, cadmium, chlorine, chromium, copper, cyanide, detergents, fluoride, iron, lead, magnesium, manganese, mercury, nickel, nitrate, pesticides, phosphates, potassium, radium, selenium, silica, silicate, silver, sodium, strontium, sulphates, zinc and others.

Ion Exchange Resins

Ion exchange resins do just that - they trade ions. They can remove phosphorus and add, say, sodium. Some add phosphorus and remove something else. Remember ions are charged particles. Cations (+ charge) are usually good for the aquarium; cations include calcium, strontium and others that are found in coral skeletons. Anions (- charge) usually aren't so good. Mixed Resin beds or deionizers marketed for aquarium use are OK; but do your home work.

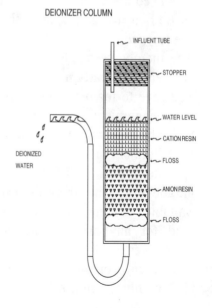

DEIONIZER COLUMN

INFLUENT TUBE
STOPPER
WATER LEVEL
CATION RESIN
FLOSS
ANION RESIN
FLOSS
DEIONIZED WATER

Some are excellent for water pretreatment only.   Others are suitable for organic removal in the saltwater aquarium. Shop wisely and be sure the resins you get will do the intended job.

The hobbyist can purchase a ready-made DI unit or purchase the resins and custom-build a DI column.

Conductivity

We will discuss conductivity in the context of checking water purity from a reverse osmosis unit or deionizing column.   Small, battery-powered conductivity meters are available to hobbyists at reasonable prices.

Conductivity is a measurement of a water sample's ability to carry, or conduct, an electrical current. Conductivity depends upon the amount of dissolved substances in the water.   It is also temperature dependent (generally, conductivity increases with higher temperatures).   It is important when comparing conductivity readings to ensure that the water sample's temperature is the same; the standard temperature is 25^0C (77^0F).   Conductivity is usually expressed as microsiemens per centimeter (μmhos/cm) at 25^0C.   As a reference, these conductivity readings are offered:

Drinking water - 50 to 1,500 μmhos/cm
"Pure" water - 10 μmhos/cm
Freshly distilled water - 0.5 to 2 μmhos/cm
Very pure water - 1 μmhos/cm
Ultrapure water - 0.1 μmhos/cm
Theoretically pure water - 0.055 μmhos/cm

A reference solution may be prepared if the hobbyist has access to a reasonably well stocked laboratory. Dissolve 0.7440 grams of potassium chloride in one liter of distilled water at 20° C (68°F.)   The conductivity of this solution (at 25°C) is about 1,410 μmhos/cm.

Algicides

Please excuse me.   I wish to state my personal opinion.   Algicides have no place in the reef aquarium. Thank you.

Algicides work very well.   That's the problem.   The chemicals that inhibit the growth of the blue-green algae ("smear" or "slime" algae) also inhibit the nitrogenous bacteria we depend on to detoxify ammonia and nitrite. Denitrifiers could also inhibit the denitrifying bacteria. Those chemicals that work on green algae also affect the zooxanthellae.   If this isn't bad enough, algae killed by algicides will release its stored nutrients as it decays. Removing the dead algae immediately and completely is necessary but not realistic.   Use nature methods to control algae after you've taken all the necessary steps to prevent its growth.

A Final Note

This is rather gross, but true, none-the-less.   The dust particles in a home's air are mostly dead skin, which, of course, contains a fair amount of phosphorus.   An air filter on the intake of a venturi protein skimmer will prevent this importation of phosphorus.

Chapter 7

FILTRATION

In this young hobby, it seems that every two years or so a "new" form of filtration is introduced. In the beginning, trickle filters were a must. Then we were introduced to the so-called "Berlin" method, which utilizes lots of live rock and protein skimming. Algae filters or "scrubbers" came along. The latest craze is the "live sand" technique. What is the hobbyist to think? The truth is, that all these systems will work; all have their strengths and weaknesses. None are perfect. The hobbyist will likely make a decision based on size - the size available for equipment under the aquarium and the size of the pocketbook.

The object of a filter is always the same. Its purpose is to remove, or convert to less objectionable forms, those compounds considered harmful to either the appearance of the aquarium or to the health of the captive animals.

The Trickle Filter

The trickle filter, or wet-dry filter, is based upon municipal sewage treatment designs of the 1920's. These filters were designed to reduce the amount of dissolved organics and ammonia/nitrite in the waste stream. The principle is simple. Polluted water is sprayed on the filter's media (which is rock in old filters and plastic media in newer ones). The decay bacteria (technically called carbonaceous bacteria) eat the dissolved carbon-based wastes and convert them to settleable particles, carbon dioxide and water or new bacteria. There are other "bugs" growing on the media as well; these are the species that convert the nitrogen-based compounds (such as ammonia, urea, nitrite, etc.) to the least objectionable form - nitrate. In a heavily stocked (and fed) aquarium, a trickle filter will act just as its industrial cousin - it converts the

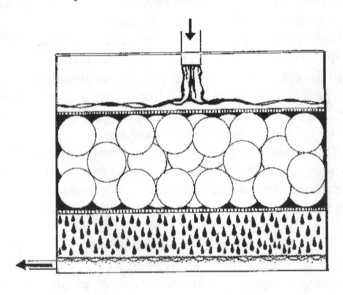

dissolved carbon-based compounds to ones that will settle in the bottom of the filter and it will produce nitrate. Unless the aeration portion (the "dry" part of the filter is pressurized, these filters will not supersaturate the water with oxygen. They will not remove the ammonia gas from solution. (There are ammonia towers, a form of trickle filter that "degas" ammonia but these work only at high pH's-

- about 10 and above). Trickle filters are OK for reef tanks if the tank contains lots of live rock (or is accompanied by a well tended, properly operating denitrification filter). Wet-drys are also very good for fish only tanks if nitrates are not a particular concern.

The "Berlin" Method

This method is so named as it originated in Berlin, Germany. It usually denotes a system using live rock as the bacterial substrate (instead of artificial plastic media) along with a protein skimmer and metal halide lighting. The protein skimmer removes, among other things, proteins which can contain about 15% nitrogen. Therefore, a protein skimmer, by removing nitrogenous compounds, lessens the amount of work the decay and nitrification bacteria must perform. The live rock bacteria can also denitrify (convert nitrates to nitrous oxide or nitrogen gas) as well as provide enough bacteria to feed the zooplankton introduced with the live rock. The commercial availability of live rock, along with sufficient lighting was a turning point for the hobby. The Berlin method is a logical extension and seems to be the choice set-up for the advanced hobbyist. It should be noted that the protein skimmers used in the Berlin Method are very large - usually 15 centimeters (6 inches) in diameter and at least 30 centimeters (one foot) in height for about every 114 liters (30 gallons) of aquarium volume. Several fellow hobbyists have noted that a very large protein skimmer makes the tank's water very stable - large amounts of kalkwasser can be added without"blasting" the pH through the roof and large water changes can be made without significantly lowering the redox value. A good skimmer will be clear so that the hobbyist can observe the bubble size (which should be no larger than the head of a safety pin).

Types of Protein Skimmers

Protein skimmers, or foam fractionators, are relatively simple devices. They are usually round containers which contain aquarium water through which air, in the form of tiny bubbles, is injected by one of several means. As these bubbles rise through the water column, they develop an electrostatic charge to which pollutants (which have an opposite charge) are attracted and "stick". At the top of the protein skimmer, these pollutants concentrate and overflow into a collection cup. In this manner, the many undesirable substances are effectively removed from the aquarium.

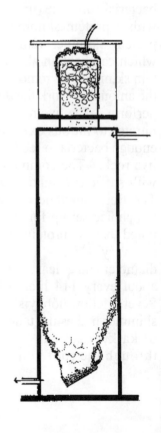

There are quite a few skimmers on the market - which is best?

There are two just rules - research your needs and buy the best skimmer that you can afford. Secondly, any properly operated and maintained skimmer is better than no skimmer at all.

A review of the protein skimmer terminology is offered to assist the hobbyist in making an educated decision when purchasing a protein skimmer.

Internal and External Skimmers

Quite simply, an internal skimmer hangs inside the aquarium or sump; an external skimmer does not and is located outside the aquarium. An internal skimmer is usually smaller than an external one, but do not make judgment by size alone. There are some very efficient internal skimmers on the market.

Co-Current and Counter-Current Skimmers

Co-current means "with the current". In this case, the current is the rising air bubbles. Therefore, aquarium water enters the cocurrent skimmer is at the bottom. Counter-current skimmers have the water entering at or near the top of the reaction tube and the water is forced downwards through the column of air bubbles which tends to increase efficiency.

Power Skimmers

"Power Skimming" is a term that is not as widely used as it once was. If a water pump is used to deliver water to, or from, the fractionator, then it is considered "powered". Most offered for sale today are power skimmers. If an air pump is used to deliver water to, or from, the skimmer, it is not considered "powered".

Air Stone versus Venturi Protein Skimmers

"Air stones" is a misnomer as they are more likely to be made of hardwood or ceramic materials. Whatever the case, they are supplied air by an electric air pump. Tiny holes in the wood or ceramic air stone break the air into small bubbles. For years, most skimmers used air stones and air pumps. These types are still available and are generally the least expensive of all skimmers. There are drawbacks - the air pump must be rebuilt periodically; that is, the diaphragms and other parts must be occasionally replaced to maintain peak efficiency. Air stones too must be replaced from time to time. They are generally "good" for 4 to 8 weeks before the tiny pores begin to clog and prevent proper air flow. If the clogged air stone is not replaced, the skimmer will obviously not be as effective in removing wastes. In addition, the air pump will be subjected to back pressure which can possibly damage it.

A venturi, or venturi "valve", is a clever device used to fine air bubbles to the skimmer. (Venturis should be familiar to us - the carburetor on a motor is a venturi in which air and fuel are mixed.) A venturi is a hollow tube with constrictions within it and, at these constrictions, is an air inlet. Venturis for aquarium applications use a motive force (water) to pass through the device's constrictions which are engineered to produce a pressure drop on the water discharge side. This pressure drop "pulls" air through the air inlet to produce tiny bubbles. The amount of air drawn through the venturi is dependent upon the rate of water flow and pressure drop or delta pressure. If we know the volume of water passing through the device and install gages on the influent and effluent sides of the venturi, then we can estimate the amount of air "pulled" through the venturi. Most hobbyists won't go to this trouble but the lesson is obvious - more gallons per minute of water going through the venturi usually means more cubic feet of air delivered to the skimmer. Venturis are generally maintenance free but should be easily removed as they do need cleaning occasionally. A venturi can be used to inject carbon dioxide or ozone if the hobbyist wishes to do so. A venturi on a larger skimmer is a very effective means of adding these gases to the aquarium water, after all, that is what they were designed to do. Venturis are often used to inject chlorine or ozone at water treatment plants.

A New Skimmer Design

A new design of protein skimmer has recently appeared on the market. It is an external, powered fractionator that uses neither air pumps or venturis. It operates on the principle that falling water creates a downdraft of air. The air to converted to fine air bubbles in a downdraft tube and is collected, along with the wastes, in a standard collection cup. These appear to be a promising advance. However, at present, they are expensive.

Is It Possible to Over-Skim?

Under normal conditions, it is not likely that an aquarium can be overskimmed but if the fractionator is oversized, redox levels can be elevated to a point (greater than 500 mV) where some corals will react negatively. The exact cause of the elevated redox is not presently known, but it is not related to oxygen levels.

Protein skimmers will also remove minerals and metals from the water. I had a metal analyses performed on some of the "gunk" collected in a large skimmer and it was found to contain calcium, strontium and an array of other elements. It is possible that these metals and minerals were bound in bacteria or suspended matter. This doesn't make a difference. A protein skimmer should be viewed as an exporter of minor and trace elements. Performing regular water exchanges should prevent these elements from being depleted.

In closing, if you choose to use the Berlin method, get the biggest protein skimmer you can afford and the premium grade live rock in sufficient quantities. Don't skimp. Metal halide lighting is often associated with this method also. This probably isn't necessary as long as enough VHO fluorescent lights are used in the halides place. See Chapter 8 for details.

Live Sand Filtration

The latest trend in reef keeping is the live sand method. It is a further extension of the Berlin method. In live sand tanks, a false, perforated bottom supports several inches of graded coral sand. (Don't collect or buy silica or "beach" sand, these may lack calcium and other elements that are beneficial.) To prevent anaerobic conditions and toxic hydrogen sulfide gas production, the sand is worked by a variety of animals (burrowing fishes, brittle stars - take care to feed them a piece of shrimp once in a while or they'll eat your snails, sea cucumbers, sand dollars, etc.). This constant working of the sand by living creatures is referred to as bioturbation.

These tanks are touted to keep nitrates at low levels. This indicates a couple of things - the amount of nitrogenous wastes in a "live rock" aquarium was overloaded by the amount of wastes produced and (2) the surface area offered by the live sand is of sufficient proportions to allow the growth of the decay-nitrifying-denitrifying bacterial populations. Further, there is good evidence that a much larger population of tiny food organisms are present. The live sand method approaches the natural reef environment where waste products are recycled, that is, converted to fatty acids, proteins and vitamins by natural bacteria which in turn are eaten by tiny protozoa that swarm out of the sand at night to become a potential food source for corals. The bacterial actions produce acids which dissolve a small portion of the coral sand. It is believed that the aquarium is naturally buffered in this manner and trace elements are slowly and naturally released. In addition, the white substrate is a good reflector and bounces light upwards thus increasing the amount of light available to the corals. Time will tell if this method is as good as it now appears.

Algae Filtration

Algae filtration is another method adapted for the aquarium from the pollution control industry, although it does mimic the algae "turfs" found naturally on the reefs. In the treatment of sewage, water hyacinths are usually employed as a form of tertiary treatment i.e., nutrient (nitrogen, phosphorus) and heavy metal removal. These will most likely be removed by aquarium algae filters as well.

Algae will produce certain substances (metabolites) and release a portion to the water. Some algae produce alcohols, some carbohydrates, etc. These substances will tend to yellow the water unless steps (water exchanges, use of activated carbon) are taken to prevent it. Some hobbyists swear by algae filtration; some swear at it. There are some very successful applications of this technology.

Fluidized Bed Filtration

The fluidized bed "filter" is a relatively new entry to the aquarium industry. Its operation is simple - a strong flow of water is introduced into the bottom of a container filled with fine sand or similar materials. The water flow is strong enough to suspended - or fluidize - the sand and it appears to "boil" in an almost hypnotic fashion. Waste-eating bacteria coat each sand particle and are constantly bathed with an oxygenated flow of water and food. The dissolved carbon compounds are converted to settleable matter (or to "new" bugs) and ammonia and nitrite should be converted to nitrate. Interestingly, if the sand bed is deep enough, or if there were to be a second fluidized bed, it might be possible to convert nitrates to nitrogen gas. It is also conceivable that phosphorus too could be removed but this would require alternating sand beds after nitrification occurs. "Luxury uptake" of phosphorus is being done on industrial scales; it will be scaled down someday.

In a sense, this type of filtration combines the best features of sand filters and trickle filters.

Activated Carbon

If you've been in the hobby for a while, you may remember activated carbon as the "charcoal" that went along with the spun-glass "floss" in the little corner filter. The charcoal was advertised to remove "harmful substances" and would relieve us from making the water exchanges. Many of us did not question these wild claims. When we set up a saltwater aquarium, we still used the charcoal (but being more sophisticated, we called it activated carbon) to remove the "harmful substances". We heard it would remove "trace elements" (whatever those were). We noticed that activated carbon would remove substances that made the water appear yellow. The water also smelled "cleaner". Then came reef aquaria. We called activated carbon "GAC" (for granular activated carbon). Many claims would be made. Some said use GAC in great quantities. Others said to use small amounts continuously. Others said use it intermittently. What should we believe?

Activated carbon is manufactured from many different substances. Coal, wood, bone, nut shells, sugar cane pulp and even manure can be used. Any of these materials can be specially treated - activated - to create a vast network of internal pores. This activation process consists of two steps. First, the organic base material is crushed, molded or extruded to the desired shape and is dehydrated. Zinc chloride or phosphoric acid are sometimes used as dehydrating agents. The particles are heated in the absence of air to 400^0C-600^0C which converts the organic material to primary and crystalline carbon along with a mixture of ash, tar and other decomposition products. A second step, activation, occurs at temperatures of 750°C-950°C while exposing the carbon to steam or carbon dioxide. Activation burns off the material clogging some of the internal pores while the pores that weren't clogged are enlarged. Macro-pores are larger than 1000 angstroms; micro-pores are smaller. (An angstrom is about 1/250,000,000ths of an inch).

Characteristics of Activated Carbon

What should an aquarist look for when purchasing GAC? Unfortunately, few clues are apparent to the eye; however, the carbon should appear to be "dull" -not glossy- and it should be dry (pay for carbon, not water). A good grade carbon should list some or all of the following information:

Surface Area (SA) or Total Surface Area (TSA): Since adsorption of organic (and inorganic) materials is a surface phenomenon, SA or TSA tells us the surface area available for this to occur. Typically, TSA is 500 to 1,400 square meters per gram of GAC. In special cases, some carbons offer 2,500 square meters/gram. Look for a high range TSA.

Iodine Number: This is a laboratory test which determines the ability of the GAC to adsorb low molecular weight substances. Typical (and acceptable) iodine numbers are 650 to 1,000.

Molasses Number: This lab test tells us the ability of the carbon to adsorb high weight molecular substances. Look for a high molasses number (greater than 500).

Other Considerations

GAC is effective at a pH range of 6.5 to 9.0 although it tends to be more effective at the lower end of the scale. At a pH of above 9, desorption of collected organics will occur. Therefore, GAC should be used upstream of any kalkwasser (lime water) additions.

Temperature also affects the adsorption abilities of GAC; it is more effective at higher temperatures.

Carbon left for a period of time in an aquarium will be colonized by various bacteria. These bacteria will utilize some of the collected materials as a food source. Instead of clogging the GAC, the bacteria will actually regenerate it to a small degree.

Can GAC Be Regenerated?

Unless the hobbyist has access to some sophisticated equipment, the answer is "no". It is best to replace (or use) carbon when the water takes on a very slight yellowish coloration.

Chapter 8

LIGHTING THE
REEF AQUARIUM

Years ago, lighting an aquarium was simple; just situate it near a window. It could be enjoyed while there was sufficient daylight available. Things got a little more complicated when incandescent and fluorescent lights became available. But there was an unwritten rule-of-thumb: incandescent for fresh-water and fluorescent for saltwater. Today, the beginning aquarist is bombarded with full page, color advertisements touting the latest and greatest in aquarium lighting technology. Sure, these lights will do the job. The truth is that almost any light (within reason) will do the job. Efficiency is the key. The system should deliver enough "light" to promote photosynthesis. Some lights are much more efficient at doing this than others. In a similar vein, over-lighting the aquarium may harm captive corals through photoinhibition. As can be imagined, over-lighting can be an expensive proposition. The lighting system for your aquarium should be considered an investment and the operating costs should be considered. Quartz lights are available at most home improvement centers. They're cheap and produce lots of light. The light is poor in the blue end of the spectrum, but rich in the yellow to red end. They will grow algae that do not need a great deal of light.

And, if there were enough of them to produce sufficient amounts of the blue-green portion of the spectrum, and corals could survive the adjustment period to this light, then the aquarist could say that a degree of success had been achieved. He would proudly point to the chiller that is necessary to maintain the water temperature at an acceptably low temperature. He would not discuss his electric utility bill.

Before investigating the pros and cons of aquarium lighting, we should acquaint ourselves with some of the terminology used in the lighting business.

Color Temperature: Color temperature is an important concept for the reef hobbyist to understand. We could use terms such as chromaticity but, unless you're a lighting engineer, why bother? Color temperature describes the apparent "whiteness" of a bulb and how natural it makes the lighted object appear. Some light bulbs make objects appear yellow (or orange or red) and these bulbs are described as being "warm." Other bulbs may make objects appear blue-white or blue or some similar color and these bulbs are described as being "cool." Color temperature (the degree of "warmness" or "coolness") is expressed in Kelvins (abbreviated as "K") on the Kelvin scale. Since most corals are found in waters that appear blue, we should choose those "cool" bulbs with a high Kelvin rating of about 5500 K or higher. A lower Kelvin rating indicates that the light is too warm or yellow. We should note that as a bulb ages, its K rating will shift to the warm end of the Kelvin scale.

The important things to remember about Color Temperature - the higher the K rating, the cooler the light appears. Choose bulbs that have a Kelvin rating of at least 5500 K. There are some metal halide bulbs appearing on the market that are 20,000 K, which is extremely blue in appearance. Bulbs lose their ratings as they age, some more so than others. See recommendations for replacing bulbs later in this chapter.

Another often used term is CRI, or Color Rendering Index. This is a scale of 0-100 and indicates how "natural" an object appears under artificial lighting. Generally, the higher the CRI number, the better the color rendering properties of the light source. CRI means a lot to those hobbyists with fish-only displays; the fish will appear more colorful under lights with high CRI's. In a reef tank, CRI doesn't mean as much because we want to use lights that will promote photosynthesis. In fact, those bulbs most efficient at promoting photosynthesis usually do not even carry a CRI rating because they weren't designed to make objects appear natural. Actinic fluorescent bulbs, which are extremely blue and have a very high Kelvin rating, are recommended for reef aquaria but would have a lousy CRI rating. Don't worry too much about CRI when choosing lights for the reef aquarium.

Lumens: Lumens measure the amount of light the human eye can see. A high lumen rating will indicate that the lighted object can be seen easily and nothing more. A lumen rating will not describe how well the light promotes photosynthesis. If it did, we could use the quartz lights that sell for less than $10 over our reef tanks.

Photosynthetically Active Radiation: Abbreviated as P.A.R., this term is widely used in horticultural literature and describes the amount of radiation available from a particular light source that promotes photosynthesis. Scientists use P.A.R. readings rather than lumens or lux.   A P.A.R. or quantum meter costs more than $1,000.   I bought one in order to judge the efficiency of various lights (and some lights are much more efficient at producing P.A.R. than others).   See Appendix.

Generally, there are two light sources available to the reef hobbyist - fluorescent tubes and metal halide bulbs.

Fluorescent Lights

Fluorescent bulbs are perhaps the most common light sources for aquaria.   These lights were first introduced in 1938, and are available today in a wide variety of "colors." In fact, there are over twenty different "white" fluorescents on the market.   Considered to be efficient lights, they produce 2 1/2 to 3 times more light than a standard incandescent bulb, while lasting 20 times longer.   Fluorescent tubes

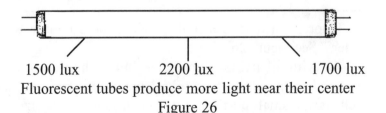

1500 lux   2200 lux   1700 lux
Fluorescent tubes produce more light near their center
Figure 26

contain argon, neon, krypton and mercury vapor sealed in a low pressure vacuum. When power is supplied, an electrical arc shoots from an electrode to an electrode at the opposite end of the tube. Initially, invisible ultra-violet (UV) light is produced. Very quickly, this UV radiation "excites" a mixture of phosphors within the tube that reemit the UV as visible light. By carefully blending phosphors, the lamp manufacturer can tailor the spectrum of the light. Table 8 lists different mixtures.

Table 8		
Fluorescent Phosphors		
Phosphor/ Activator	Wavelength Peak	Color
Calcium Tungstate/Lead	440nm	Blue
Strontium Cholorapatite/Europium	445 nm	Blue
Barium Titanium Phosphate/Titanium	490 nm	Blue-Green
Zinc Sulfate/Manganese	520 nm	Green
Magnesium Fluorogermanate/Manganese	660 nm	Red

Fluorescent tubes generally produce more light at the center. See Figure 26.

As with all lights, fluorescent bulbs should not be expected to maintain their initial lumen output. With each start, a small portion of the electrodes is vaporized.

This becomes visible as black bands at each end of the tube. Standard, four foot 40-watt tubes and High Output (HO) bulbs drop to about 80% of initial lumens in about 3000 hours of operating time. These numbers are based on industry standard operational periods of three hours each.

Realistically, the bulb can be expected to last slightly longer. Very High Output (VHO) fluorescents lose efficiency more quickly. If we follow the recommendations of horticulturists and replace lights when they reach 70% of initial lumen output, we can expect to change fluorescent bulbs every 6 to 9 months. If they are supplemental light to another light source, such as a metal halide, the expected life can be extended by a month or so.

Fluorescents are designed to operate at maximum efficiency when the coolest part of the bulb is 104°F. It seems that temperature affects the operating pressure within the lamp. Operating the bulb above or below this temperature can drastically affect the lumen output. For instance, only 80% of the manufacturers stated initial lumens will be produced by a new bulb operating at 60°F; 90% of initial lumens will be produced by the same bulb at 120° F.

Fluorescents are available in a variety of diameters. The most efficient of these are the T12 tubes (T means "tubular" and 12 represents the bulb diameter in eighths of an inch; 12/8ths = 1 1/2 inches). T8's (1 inch diameter) are the next most efficient size.

Some fluorescent tubes contain internal reflectors. A white powder layer between the glass envelope and the phosphors effectively bounces the light towards the aquarium

They are said to be more efficient and are slightly more expensive. Dimming of fluorescents is possible and several methods of doing so exists. All dimmers reduce electrical current through the lamp. Be aware that fluorescent dimmers offer reductions in light down to about 1% of operating lumens - they do not dim to no light at all.

Metal Halide Lights

The metal halide bulb is a relatively new introduction that was designed to provide natural appearing light for applications such as television studios. They, along with mercury vapor and high pressure sodium lamps, are known as High Intensity Discharge (HID) lamps.

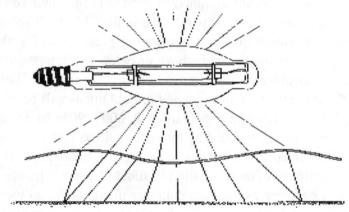

Figure 27

Metal halides for the aquarium trade usually consist of an outer bulb and an inner bulb or arc tube. Within the arc tube are electrodes and the elements mercury, argon and metal halides.

These halides are forms of metals that vaporize at temperatures lower than the metals themselves would. This is fortunate, as the glass envelopes would melt at the metal's vaporization temperature. Halides such as scandium, thorium and dysprosium produce a wide spectrum of light at operating temperature, while others, such as indium, produce very narrow line spectrums. Indium peaks at 435 nm, which is blue. The amount of mercury within the arc tube determines the operating pressure and, to some degree, the color of the radiant energy. Operating a metal halide designed for horizontal operation in a vertical position alters the arc length and operating pressure within the arc tube and therefore alters the Kelvin rating.

Metal halides operate at high temperatures and their electrodes evaporate more quickly than other light sources. This heat can cause other failures due to softening of the glass and solder. Corrosion of the mogul base is a another cause of failure. Generally, metal halides reach 70% of initial lumens in about 8,000 to 10,000 hours of operation. A shift in the spectrum from blue to orange can also be expected.

Dimming of metal halides is possible. Dimmers reduce the voltage or current through the arc tube. As the voltage is reduced, some of the halides cannot stay vaporized and the radiated color shifts. At about 60% lumen output, the spectrum emitted will be very similar to a mercury vapor light: it will be distinctly blue-green.

Since metal halides are excellent point sources of light, they can produce very desirable light patterns in the aquarium. When sufficient water movement produces surface ripples or waves, the light is diffused by the concave portion of the wave or concentrated by the convex pattern. In effect, the wave acts as a magnifying glass, which focuses the light on the substrate. These focused and diffused light patterns are called "glitter lines." See Figure 27. The symbiotic zooxanthellae within the coral's tissue may benefit from these light pulses.

Lighting System Maintenance

It's just a fact of life that clean things eventually get dirty and aquarium lights and the light fixture units (properly called luminaires) are no exceptions. To keep your lighting system at peak efficiency, it is a good idea to develop a maintenance schedule and stick with it.

Maintenance for Luminaires

The amount of dirt accumulated on the luminaire reflective surface can greatly affect the amount of light reaching the aquarium. Dirt causes an absorption of light and can alter the light distribution patterns and spectral quality. Two reflective surfaces are generally available: polished aluminum and aluminum coated with white enamel. Clean polished aluminum with mild soap and water and rinse immediately with clean fresh water. Avoid strong alkaline cleaners. For enamels, use mild soap and water while carefully avoiding alcohols, abrasive or aggressive cleaners.

Cleaning the Luminaire Lens and Lamps

A luminaire will usually have a protective lens for a couple of reasons. It will keep foreign matter (such as salt spray) off the hot bulbs and, if so equipped, allow a cooling fan to create a good cross ventilation that would "short circuit" without the lens. Over a short period of time, a thin film of dirt and dust will coat the lens. Plastic lens are noted for their ability to collect dust as they become charged with static electricity. For these reasons, the lens should be removed periodically months and cleaned. Do so with mild detergent and water. Do not use abrasive cleaners. Rinse with clean fresh water and, to avoid scratching, allow to drip dry or blot dry with a clean, lint-free rag. While the lens is off, it is a good idea to clean the bulbs, as well. This is especially important for fluorescent bulbs since some types are coated with silicone to provide quick starts in humid conditions and dirt negates this feature. Turn the lamps off and allow sufficient time to cool to room temperature. Wipe fluorescents with a soft, dry cloth to clean. Metal halides can also be wiped clean and, if the dirt is really stubborn, use commercial glass cleaner. Carefully inspect all bulbs for cracks, loose end caps or mogul bases or any other obvious signs of wear or damage. Avoid scratching any bulb while cleaning.

Notes on Factors Affecting Light Transmission

It is very important that the top of the aquarium, if it has one, be kept clean. A quick check with a light meter found $3/8$ ths plexiglas coated with a thin dust layer and salt spray reduced light transmission by 14%. An equally unclean piece of 3/8ths glass reduced light transmission by 20%. Keep these surfaces clean!

In another experiment, the water in a 70-gallon aquarium was tinted with yellow food coloring until it would not pass a commercially available "carbon tester." Light transmission was reduced by a further 8%. Since water yellowing affects both the transmission and spectral quality of the light as it passes through the water, take measures to keep the yellow out. Regular use of activated carbon and water exchanges should accomplish this under normal circumstances.

Which Lighting System Is Best?

This question is easy to answer - it depends. Obviously, if the aquarium houses only shade-loving corals such as Tubastraea, sufficient light for viewing purposes is all that is needed. On the other hand, a tank simulating a reef flat inhabited by Honeycomb (Goniastrea) and Staghorn (Acropora) corals will need a terrific amount of light.

Although sunlight would be the best light to use, few of us can take advantage of it as a main light source unless we live near the equator. At subtropical and temperate latitudes the seasonal variations in solar radiation make the sun a supplemental light source at best.

Realistically, fluorescents and metal halides will be the choices for the aquarist. Before interpreting the results of some decidedly tedious testing, we must realize that many variables come into play that may affect the amount of light actually reaching a coral. Some of these are:

1. Age of the bulb
2. Height of the bulb above the water's surface
3. Type of ballast used
4. Line voltage
5. Cleanliness of the luminaire
6. Cleanliness and type of lens (if any)
7. Cleanliness of the bulb
8. Type of reflective surface in the luminaire
9. Aquarium construction (bracing, glass or acrylic top)
10. Operating temperature of the bulb
11. Operating position of the bulb
12. Reflectance of water's surface
13. Water clarity (yellowing)
14. Amount of suspended material in the water column
15. Color of the aquarium background
16. Color of the substrate
17. Slight manufacturing differences from bulb to bulb
18. Quality and condition of the light metering equipment

For those interested, the testing protocol and complete results of the lighting tests will be listed in the Appendix.

Condensed Results of Light Tests

Fluorescent Lights
Average Readings
4- 110 watt VHOs (2 actinic, 2 "reef" bulbs)
Just below surface- 9992 lux
6" deep- 9671 lux
12" deep- 8437 lux
Bottom (18")- 7294 lux

2- 110 watt VHOs ("reef" bulbs)
Just below surface- 6811 lux
6" deep- 5858 lux
12" deep- 5753 lux
Bottom (18")- 5253 lux

Metal Halide Bulbs
2 - 175 watt bulbs
Average Readings
Just below surface- 16,686 lux
6" deep- 14,481 lux
12" deep- 13,278 lux
Bottom (18")- 12,293 lux

Photosynthetically Active Radiation

Metal halide lighting would seem to be the light of choice if we judge strictly by lux or lumen readings. However, not all light is equal in stimulating photosynthesis. In order to evaluate the effectiveness of different lights, we'll use a measure of radiation called Photosynthetically Active Radiation (PAR), which is measured in quanta units called microEinsteins as measured over area units and time units (usually quanta per square meter per second). This is abbreviated as µE m s. The higher the reading the higher the amount of PAR.

By using conversion factors, the aquarist can estimate the amount of "usable" light reaching the corals. Scientists have determined that, in nature, corals usually need PAR ranging from 30 to 1780 µE m s. We will examine the specific needs of coral species in Chapters 10 - 30.

Estimations of PAR for Different Lights
Average microEinsteins per square meter per second

Fluorescents

```
2 - 110 watt "Reef" Bulbs
Just below surface- 127
6" deep - 109
12" deep - 108
Bottom (18") - 98
```

```
4 -110 watt VHOs - 2 actinic, 2 "reef" bulbs
Just below surface - 431
6" deep - 396
12" deep - 335
Bottom (18") - 270
```

```
Metal Halides - 2-175 watt bulbs
Just below surface - 222
6" deep - 192
12" deep - 176
Bottom - 163
```

Chapter 9

CREATING CURRENTS

"Don't make waves." We've all been given that advice at one time or another. Ignore it. Make waves. Your corals will appreciate it. So will your fishes. And it will make tank maintenance easier.

Types of Water Motion

In nature, water currents are produced by winds, tides, temperature differences, etc. None of these are any good at producing significant water currents in the aquarium and artificial means must be employed. Some means are excellent at producing a certain forms of water movement, while being poor at others. The three types of water motion that interest us are laminar flow, turbulent flow and surge. Laminar flow is flow that varies little in either direction or velocity. Turbulent flow is the opposite of laminar flow. Turbulent flow varies erratically in velocity and direction. Surge is a sweeping motion of water that often accompanies waves.

Laminar Flow

Laminar flow is perhaps the easiest to produce in an aquarium. Powerheads or other small pumps can provide it.

So can filtration system pump effluent flows. Fishes enjoy this type of movement if it is not too strong and is fairly localized. Many fishes will "play" in this type of current and will swim in and out of it. They get exercise and it is quite amusing to watch. Do corals need this flow? In nature, shallow water corals experience quite strong laminar flow with each changing of the tide. In fact, some corals with tightly spaced, finger-like branches likely require laminar flow to provide food and carry wastes and other detritus away. Other corals, such as Tubastraea, also require this flow for the same reasons. Some studies suggest that coral skeletal calcification decreases along with flow rates.

Alternating Laminar Flow

Several methods for alternating current exist. The first, and most expensive, is a timer/alternator electrical relay that controls water flow through two or more pipes. The actual control device is usually a motorized ball valve that opens or closes upon command from the timer. In a two pipe system, water is pumped through the pipe and open ball valve until the timer tells the valve to close. The timer tells the other valve to open at the same time. This method is for "gadget freaks" with deep pockets and a willingness to stock spare parts. A more reasonable method is one of the commercially available "wave makers." The name is a misnomer as these don't actually make waves but, more closely simulate, the flow associated with tidal changes. Good units are electrically grounded, can power four powerheads or similar pumps, and have variable cycle times with a manual delay to use while feeding the tank.

These are neat items. The third alternative is perhaps the best and least expensive. Inexpensive timers made for household use (available at the hardware store for about $10 each) control the pumps. The beauty of this set-up is that the circulation pumps are individually timed. They can be run all at once or not at all. If correctly done, these can produce laminar flow to closely approximate the "rushing" and ebb of the tides. If aimed correctly, they can also produce turbulent flow.

Turbulent Flow

As we just noted, turbulent flow can be produced with some common aquarium pumps. For a little more money, there are some imported pumps that have variable speed control. Combine these with any sort of timing device and the aquarist can spend the rest of his days investigating the various possibilities.

Surge

Surge is not commonly seen in home aquariums although it is not particularly difficult to produce. There are surge making devices marketed as "algae scrubbers." Hobbyist magazines routinely carry "how-to" articles on constructing inexpensive surge-making devices. Is surge necessary? Almost every coral is exposed to it in nature. In the aquarium, the sweeping or rocking surge action keeps the fleshy tentacles of corals, such as Euphyllia and Goniopora, in constant motion. Surge buckets or dump buckets also produce small (about 1 inch) waves.

These waves act as magnifying glasses and concentrate the light beams (especially those of metal halides) into"caustic networks"(sometimes referred to as"glitter lines"), which travel the length of the aquarium. Since the coral tentacles are rocking back and forth, the entire tentacle is, at one time or another, subjected to the intensified light and its useful radiation. In fact, experiments with plankton and pulsed, blue light similar to that produced by the combination of sun and wave action, found photosynthesis to be increased by as much as 30% in some cases.

Recommended water motion for individual coral species will be discussed in Chapters 10 to 30.

PART THREE
CORALS

Chapter 10

The Mushroom Polyps
ACTINODISCUS

Pronounced Ak-tin-oh-dis-kus

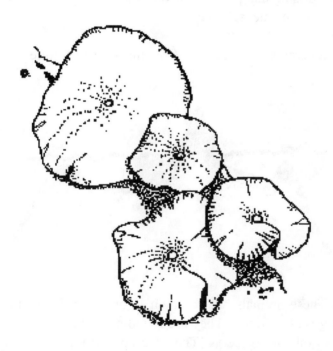

These animals are not really corals, but, are instead, corallimorpharia - "false corals." These rather attractive creatures are frequently available and may be sold as "mushroom" corals or "mushroom rock." Often, an Actinodiscus colony may consist of 40 or more individual animals on a small piece of live rock. Coloration varies: some may be reddish-brown, blue or striped green and brown. Others may be a multi-colored marbleized pattern, which is especially attractive under blue actinic light. It is not surprising that price often varies according to the beauty of the specimens.

Where Do Actinodiscus Colonies Live in Nature?

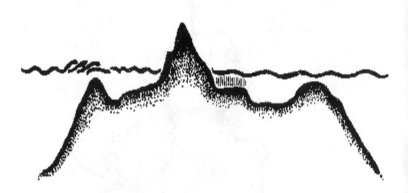

These animals are common in areas, sheltered from strong wave action. They are found at depths of up to 20 meters (about 66 feet). The geographical range stretches from the Red Sea, southward and eastwards through the Indo-Pacific and Coral Sea.

Lighting Requirements

These false corals contain the symbiotic zooxanthellae, but can survive with relatively little light. Although they can do quite well under four 40-watt fluorescent tubes, a 175-watt metal halide bulb with supplemental actinic fluorescent lights is a better choice. By merely increasing the amount of light over an Actinodiscus colony, I observed the animals to begin reproducing via the asexual means known as budding.

Feeding

Some Actinodiscus can apparently survive on the translocated zooxanthellae metabolites and dissolved organic matter absorbed from the water column. Others seem to appreciate occasional feedings. The hobbyist is advised to offer these animals small pieces of shrimp, squid or other foodstuffs of oceanic origin. A feeding response is indicated when the animal closes into a tear-drop shape. If this is the case with your captive false corals, then all means offer foods every few days.

Water Currents

Since these animals are found in sheltered reef areas, it is not surprising that a gentle current is all that is required for these creatures well-being. A small powerhead may be all that is required.

A Final Note

See Chapter 32 for a brief listing of Actinodiscus predators.

Chapter 11

The Star Polyps
CLAVULARIA
Pronounced Clav-u-larry-ah

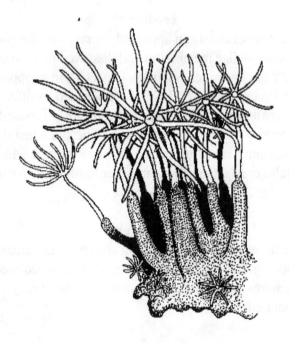

Few corals can rival the beauty of a colony of Green Star Polyps (Clavularia viridis) when viewed under actinic fluo-rescent lighting.   The intensely green glow of these animals' ultraviolet radiation absorbing compounds almost defies description.   Fortunately, Star Polyps are commonly available and are quite hardy in captivity.   They are highly recommended to the beginning hobbyist.

Where Do Clavularia Colonies Live in Nature?

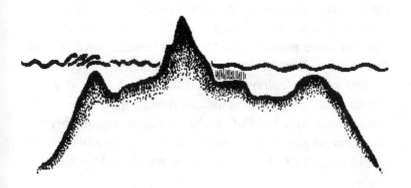

Clavularia colonies are often found in shallow waters sheltered from strong wave action and near land masses. These waters are often turbid and laden with organic materials due to run-off from the land.   Colonies prefer to grow on hard substrates or rubble bottoms.   .
These animals are common throughout the tropical Pacific Ocean.

Lighting Requirements

These octocorals do not seem particular as to the amount of light they receive. Growing colonies have been noted under two 40-watt actinic and two 40-watt daylight fluorescent tubes (providing 140 µEinsteins per square meter per second). Superior growth rates can be achieved with a combination of metal halide lamps and actinic fluorescent tubes.

Water Currents

If Clavularia colonies seem undemanding in their lighting requirements, the same cannot be said about the amount of water flow they prefer. Too little flow seems to smother these animals and they may become covered with sheets of red or blue-green cyanobacteria. Too much current and the colony may fail to expand fully, if at all. Proper water movement is indicated when the colony gently waves much as a field of grain ripples in a gentle breeze. As a general guideline, proper water flow rates will be in the neighborhood of 8 to 10 centimeters (3 to 4 inches) per second.

Feeding

Many Star Polyp colonies seem to do fine with no special feeding. In fact, scientists have debated if these animals need any feeding at all. They've noted that the digestive organelles have degenerated almost to the point of uselessness. Combined with the fact that feeding behavior is only rarely seen, it would seem possible that they get most (or all) of their nutrition from their symbiotic zooxanthellae. However, it is also probable that carbon and organic nitrogen and phosphorus are obtained through absorption or by ingesting bacteria or microscopic animals such as protozoa.

Mineral/Metal Requirements

Since these animals contains tiny calcium reinforcing rods called spicules, it will be necessary to monitor the aquarium water for calcium content with a calcium test kit and make calcium additions as needed. Strontium may also be required. No Test kits exists for this element; periodic additions of a commercially available strontium supplement should be made. Follow the directions on the bottle. Making regular, partial water exchanges will keep a supply of various elements available for the zooxanthellae. These water exchanges will usually decrease the chance of algae growth, which can smother and kill a Clavuaria colony.

Chapter 12

The Cabbage Corals

LOBOPHYTUM

Pronounced Low-bow-fye-tum

With a lot of imagination, this soft coral might resemble a head of cabbage. It is also sold under the equally undescriptive name of "Wall coral." Names of this type make a strong argument for the hobbyist to be familiar with, and use the Latin names.

While these corals are not particularly exotic, they are reasonably hardy and offer a rather unique presence to the reef aquarium. Small specimens are not uncommon in well-stocked pet shops. In nature, this animal can grow to be 1 meter (39 inches) in diameter.

Where Do Lobophytum Colonies Live in Nature?

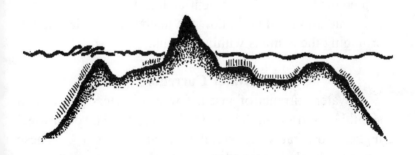

The Cabbage coral is most often found in sheltered waters with a high organic content and gentle water currents.

Shallow reef flats (less than 10 meters - 33 feet) seem to be the preferred habitat, although some low profile specimens are found on or near reef crests. These corals are abundant from the Red Sea across the Indo-Pacific to the Great Barrier Reef, the Coral Sea and beyond and north-wards to cooler waters, such as those found near Okinawa.

Lighting Requirements
This octocoral, which contains zooxanthellae, is not really demanding in its lighting needs. The standard set-up of four 40-watt fluorescent tubes (2 daylight or "reef" bulbs and 2 actinic tubes) is usually sufficient in aquariums less than 18 inches deep. Of course, metal halides supplemented with fluorescent actinic tubes will generate more radiation and will allow the hobbyist more latitude in arranging the animals within the tank.

Water Currents
Water currents of just a few centimeters per second should be sufficient. The animal will appreciate occasional higher flow rates (to simulate tidal changes). These currents should be strong enough to cleanse the coral of any detritus that may have accumulated in the its fleshy folds.

Feeding
Lobophytum corals may not need supplemental feedings if lighting is of sufficient quantity and quality. This is especially so if the aquarium also contains a few regularly-fed fishes; the fish food "scraps" will serve as a coral food.

If the animal is observed to be shrinking in size or it is losing the calcium spicules from its base, then feeding will be necessary. The coral food described in Chapter 31 should be adequate.

Since the animal contains calcium spicules, add "kalkwasser" or other calcium supplement to maintain proper calcium levels. These spicules may also contain strontium (which should also be added), manganese and other elements. Water exchanges should keep these from being depleted.

Other Notes

Lobophytum specimens often produce shiny mucus sheets that may cover the animal for weeks. Slightly increased water currents may be used to remove this sheet once it begins to loosen from the animal. Remove the mucus sheet with a net or pipette once it becomes detached. Lobophytum produces noxious chemicals (terpenes) to irritate or kill competitors for space or light and this mucus may contain small amounts.

Lobophytum can reproduce sexually and asexually. Small specimens (less than 18 centimeters - about 7 inches) across are sexually immature. There is little doubt that this coral can be propagated by asexual means. See Chapter 34 for further details.

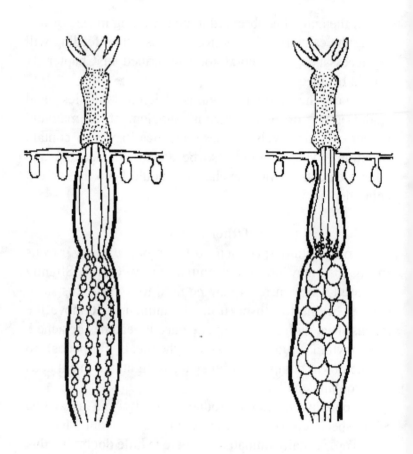

The sex organs in Lobophytum corals lie just below the animals ectoderm, or skin. A male polyp is on the left; a female colony with eggs is on the right.

Chapter 13

The Leather Corals
SARCOPHYTON
Pronounced Sar-ko-fye-ton

The Leather corals are perhaps the most popular of the soft corals. This popularity is not without good reason - they're readily available, moderately priced, extremely hardy and, with experience can be propagated in captivity. In short, specimens of the genus Sarcophyton are close to being the perfect beginner's soft coral. There interesting appearance and delicate coloration are enough to keep the advanced hobbyist's interest, as well.

Where Do Sarcophyton Corals Live in Nature?

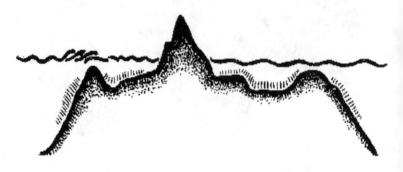

Specimens of the genus Sarcophyton are widely distributed. They are found in the Red Sea, off the east coast of Africa and westward across the Indo-Pacific. They are also abundant on Australia's Great Barrier Reef and on the countless reefs across the Coral Sea.

There are many species, some of which inhabit specific niches on the reef. These animals prefer a hard substrate, but may attach to rubble covering a soft bottom. On the Great Barrier Reef, some species live in shallow waters described as "dirty" and "algae-laden." In the Red Sea, these animals often form large "carpets" consisting of hundreds of individuals. They sometimes live on reef flats covered with the sea weed Saragassum.

That this coral can live in "dirty" water (with associated low light levels) may explain why they have high survival rates in home aquaria.

Lighting Requirements

In general, leather corals don't need a lot of light. Good results can be obtained with 4 or 6 standard 40 watt fluorescent tubes. A combination of blue actinic and daylight or "reef" bulbs will be appreciated. Of course, metal halide bulbs with supplemental blue VHO fluorescent lights work well. If these are used, the animal should be acclimated to the higher light levels by initially placing it near the bottom or in a partially shaded spot and moving it to well lighted spots over the course of 3 or 4 weeks.

Shallow-water specimens are often beige or yellow, while those from deeper waters are brown or brown-green. The symbiotic algae, zooxanthellae, is found in the tissues of healthy Sarcophyton specimens.

Water Currents

As with most fleshy soft corals, these animals don't need a great deal of water movement. However, it is important that the flow be sufficient to keep the tentacled cap free of fouling detritus. Occasional currents of 10 to 15 centimeters (4 to 6 inches) per second should satisfy this demand.

Feeding Requirements

Like many coelenterates, this coral can likely absorb dissolved organic substances from the water to supplement the nutrition obtained from the zooxanthellae's metabolites. If a few fish are kept in the aquarium, these and other corals may get sufficient nutrition from the fish food scraps.

Other Notes

Sarcophyton specimens often - sometimes weekly - retract their polyps and become covered with a shiny mucus sheet that almost appears to be made of plastic. This should not be a cause for concern. This coating will sometimes stay on the coral until it is coated with a light film of algae. Once the mucus begins to loosen, the hobbyist may hasten the process by squirting it with a small plastic kitchen baster or eye-dropper. This clear coating consists of proteins, fats and other compounds, one of which, is a terpene called Sarcophene. This chemical can irritate fish and other corals if the concentration is high enough. It's not a bad idea to remove this coating from the aquarium. See Chapter 32 for more details.

Chapter 14

The Dead Man's Hand Corals
SINULARIA

Pronounced Sin-u-larry-ah

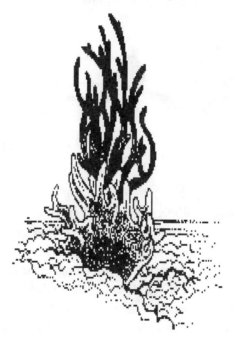

Specimens of the genus Sinularia are very common Pacific soft corals. They are fast-growing and generally do very well in reef aquaria. Their trade names are many - Leather corals, Dead Man's Hand, etc. This demonstrates the problem with using common names, since "Leather Coral" applies to at least one other genus.

Where Do Sinularia Colonies Live in Nature?

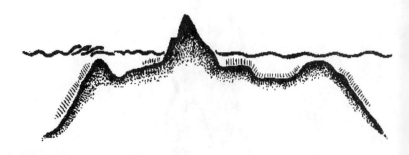

Sinularia colonies are found in just about every reef niche. Some species inhabit inshore areas and are subjected to wide swings in temperature, salinity, water flow, dissolved oxygen and other parameters. Others are found near wave-pounded reef crests, while still others live in reef flat tunnels and reef slopes. They are quite common in the Red Sea, Coral Sea, Great Barrier Reef and Indo-Pacific.

Dead Man's Hand corals often form monospecific carpets, where they may compose 80% to 90% of live coverage on hard or rubble substrates.

Different Shapes of Sinularia Colonies

Understanding the various shapes in which Sinularia colonies can be found greatly assists the aquarist in determining the animal's requirements in captivity. Those specimens appearing to be compressed in appearance are most likely shallow-water creatures subjected to at least periodic high water flow rates and relatively high light levels. If the animal is tree-like in appearance it may require less light and less, but more constant, water flow.

Lighting Requirements

It is possible to maintain specimens of this genus under standard 40-watt fluorescent tubes (4 to 6 with a 50/50 split of actinic tubes and "reef" or daylight tubes). Be certain to change the lights every six months. A luminaire containing metal halides (175-watt) produce enough light; a fixture with metal halides and two actinic tubes is an excellent choice. Like specimens of the genus Sarcophyton, these corals occasionally coat themselves with a temporary mucus sheathing that may cover the animal for up to two weeks. All tentacles will be withdrawn while coated by this mucus sheet. It is believed that this behavior is not a response to stress, but is, instead, an expulsion of excess carbon translocated from the animal's symbiotic zooxanthellae. If the animal is not periodically shedding a mucus skin, or is not growing, try increasing the light by slowly lowering the luminaire or by carefully moving the animal to an area that receives more light. Adding an addtional light is also an option.

Water Currents

General recommendations based on the shape of the specimen can be made as to the amount of water flow required. Compact forms (such as the cushion-like Sinularia dura) will likely require flow rates of 10 centimeters (4 inches) per second while tree-like forms (Sinularia flexibilis, for instance) may appreciate a flow that makes them wave slightly. Using powerheads on a "wave-maker" or individual timers can be recommended.

Metal/Mineral Requirements

Sinularia specimens contain many needle-like structures to lend rigidity to the fleshy tissues. The large needles, called spicules, may be 1 millimeter in diameter and several millimeters long. Much smaller rods called clubs also lend support. These structural components are made of calcium and magnesium and may comprise as much as 50% of the animal's dry weight. The aquarist is advised to monitor aquarium water calcium levels with a good test kit and add kalkwasser or calcium chloride as needed. Adequate magnesium levels can be maintained through regular, partial water changes.

Other Notes

This coral (like many others) contains and excretes noxious compounds, called terpenes, to avoid predation, kill or make ill competitors for space or light and prevent algae overgrowth. These compounds can be toxic to fish, as well. In addition to water changes, it is advisable to use a properly sized and maintained protein skimmer. Occasional use of granular activated carbon may also be helpful.

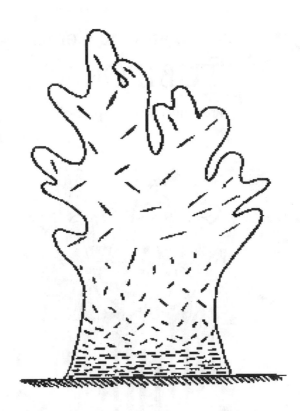

Sinularias contain hundreds of calcium reinforcing rods called clubs and spicules.

Chapter 15

The Organ Pipe Corals
TUBIPORA

Pronounced Tube-i-pore-ah

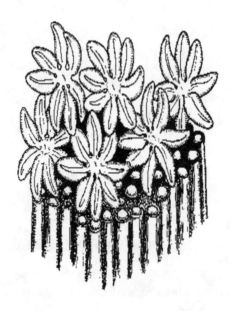

Among soft corals, Tubipora is somewhat of a contradiction, in that it builds an external calcareous skeleton. This skeleton is colored a deep red and consists of a complex of parallel tubes in which the animals live. This coral's eight tentacles are feather-like in appearance. Unlike the skeleton, this octocoral is a rather drab green or brown in color.

Where Do Tubipora Colonies Live in Nature?

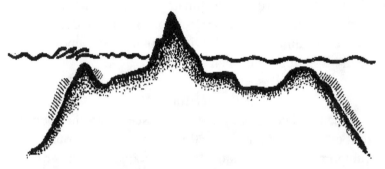

The Organ Pipe coral prefers waters with good clarity and flow rates. It is only rarely found in areas subjected to terrestrial run-off. It is often found on exposed and semi-exposed reefs to depths of about 15 meters.

Lighting Requirements

In nature, Tubipora is exposed, at a minimum, to about 400 microEinsteins per square meter per second. Two 175-watt metal halide bulbs used in conjunction with VHO actinic tubes will provide about 220 µE m s at a depth of 18 inches and will meet this animal's minimum requirements. I have used 250-watt metal halides and VHO actinics with good success.

Water Currents

Since Pipe Organ corals are from areas exposed to moderate wave action, we can expect them to enjoy water flow rates of about 10 centimeters (4 inches) per second. Some experimentation by the hobbyist may be necessary to determine the best location for this animal. Exercise caution however when moving this animal; its skeleton is fragile and easily breaks. Any tumble from its perch will likely fragment the unfortunate coral. The lesson is obvious - once a suitable location has been determined, secure the animal in place with an underwater epoxy or by gently wedging it between live rocks.

Feeding

Feed this coral once or twice a week with the food described in Chapter 31. Researchers have found that Tubipora colonies contain abnormally high amounts of fats. Though the animal's zooxanthellae may supply these lipids (or their precursors) under proper lighting, we can not rule out the possibility that they are supplied by foods such as zooplankton or a suitable substitute.

Mineral/Metal Requirements

The fused spicules forming the Tubipora skeleton are composed of mostly calcium. Strontium and magnesium may also be major components. I will speculate that the red coloration indicates a high iron content, and certainly betacarotene, as well.

If conditions are proper, this octocoral will grow rather quickly in the aquarium.

Chapter 16

The Pulse or Pom-Pom Corals
XENIA

Pronounced Zen-ee-ah

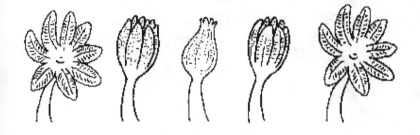

Xenia corals get their common name from the rhythmic pul-
sations of its eight feather-like tentacles. This movement is
rather unusual among corals and makes Xenia a perennial
favorite. Xenia can be distinguished from other soft corals
by its tree-like appearance; that is, they have a trunk which
sprouts many limbs.

Where Do Xenia Colonies Live in Nature?

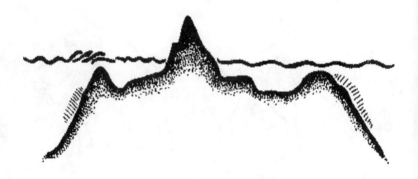

Xenia colonies are common on many reefs from the Red
Sea and across the Indian and Pacific Oceans.

As with many corals, generalizations have to be made as
to habitat. These animals are usually found on reef flats
and slopes protected from strong wave action although
some species are found in exposed areas. Habitat water
transparency can be rated as good to excellent. Xenia
colonies prefer hard substrates and can be found to depths
of about 15 meters (49 feet).

Lighting Requirements

A rather simple test exists for determining if Xenia colonies are receiving sufficient light. Some researchers have noted this coral failed to pulsate under minimal lighting and eventually died. Adequate light can be supplied for some species by 40-watt fluorescent bulbs (two actinic and two daylights). Be absolutely certain to replace these bulbs every 5 or 6 months. Success has also been noted when using a metal halide/fluorescent combination.

Water Currents

Although Xenia specimens may be found on reef areas where water currents routinely reach velocities of 20 to 30 centimeters (8 to 12 inches) per second, this is usually impractical to duplicate in display aquaria. Water returns from a circulation pump, or small powerheads, strategically placed every two feet or so should produce adequate water movement.

Feeding

Several researchers have written that Xenia is autotrophic and requires no feeding other than the foods supplied by its captive zooxanthellae. They cite that some species do not possess the nematocysts used to capture prey and have digestive tracts that have degenerated to a point of near uselessness. In addition, they may show no feeding response to amino acids, crab meat juice "labelled" with ink or any other foods for that matter. However, radioactive carbon is incorporated by the animal's zooxanthellae, suggesting that dissolved organic matter is used by the animal.

Feeding the fish in the reef tank containing Xenia specimens may be all that is required to satisfy the coral. There is some evidence that Xenia colonies need iodine supplements (which can be monitored with a colorimetric test kit).

Other Notes

When shopping for a Xenia specimen, look for polyps that are firm and not jelly-like. Ideally the polyps should be "pulsing." Shop wisely as these animals are not known to ship very well.

If the animal is not expanded, carefully inspect it for any crabs. Some crabs are parasitic and will eventually destroy the coral; others are commensal and may do no lasting harm.

Chapter 17

The Staghorn Corals
ACROPORA

Pronounced <u>Akro</u>-pore-ah

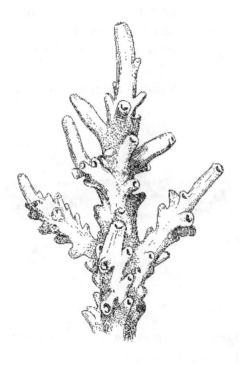

Acropora is perhaps the most well known of all corals. Little wonder, over 400 species have been described from the Atlantic, Caribbean, Indo-Pacific, south Pacific and the Red Sea.   Their success is due to their amazing adaptive abilities.   Some tortured species inhabit the most violent, surf-pounded reef crests, while others exist in tranquil lagoons.   Ironically, Acropora is noted as being a delicate creature in captivity.

Since this coral inhabits such a variety of reef environments, the aquarist most successful with this genus will have carefully studied the animal's requirements.

Where Do Acropora Colonies Live in Nature?

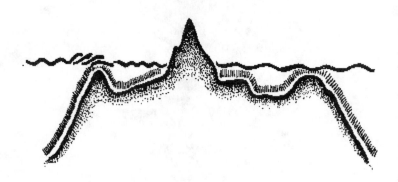

This diagram illustrates the range of natural habitats for some common Staghorn corals.

The majority of Acropora species inhabit upper reef slopes and lagoons. Of particular interest to aquarists is the loose classification of coral shape and its environment. For instance, those Acropora species subjected to the violent exposed reef crest are most likely to be very solidly built, while lagoon species are prone to widely spaced, elongated branches, which could never withstand strong currents without breaking. Therefore, very general guidelines can be made for aquarium lighting and water movement. Figure 30 depicts some of the different Acropora forms. Optimal temperature for growth is 26°C to 27°C.

Higher temperatures may stress the animal and lead to disease, such as white band disease. See Chapter 32.

Corymbose/Digitate Forms

These forms of Acropora are most often found in shallow reef environments, such as outer reef flats and upper reef slopes. In the case of the outer reef flat, the water may be so shallow that the corals are exposed (emerged) at low tide. Water clarity would be expected to be quite good (Jerlov Type II oceanic) with only small amounts of suspended matter. Any sedimentation on the coral could be expected to be washed away with currents of up to 0.6 meters (24 inches) per second. During ebb tide, currents may be as low as 3 cm (1.2 inches) per second. It is important that aquarium water movement be sufficient to remove any sedimentation from Acropora, as sedimentation between the tightly packed branches will smother the animal. We can also estimate the lighting requirements for these shallow water creatures.

Different Shapes of Acropora Corals

Table

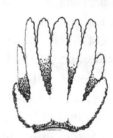
Digitate

Corymbose

Branching

Bottlebrush

Caespitose

Massive

Encrusting

Figure 30

Light intensity should be 72,000 lux (1,340 μE m s) to 96,000 lux (1,780 μE m s) - see Chapter 8. However, Acropora does not utilize this much light and, in fact, utilizes only a fraction. For instance, Acropora digitifera (a shallow water coral with short, stubby branches) will "saturate" at about 22,000 lux of sunlight; that is, the coral's zooxanthellae are photosynthesizing at a maximum rate and increasing the light will not increase the amount of translocated carbon to the coral animal. Acropora from shallow depths with strong currents will have branches that appear so:

Table or Plate Forms

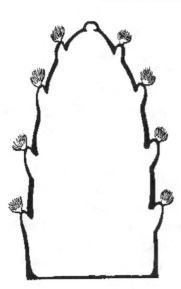

These forms of Acropora inhabit almost all reef niches. In turbulent waters, their size will be smaller (to avoid breakage) than in calmer waters. Table-like corals have the poorest ability to shed sediments, therefore, water currents in the aquarium must be strong enough to wash these away. An assumption must be made for recommendations on specimen placement in the aquarium. Since collectors will likely harvest those corals most easily collected and smaller sizes are most suitable for the reef aquarium, it would not be unreasonable to suppose that most table-like Acropora would be collected from shallow sites similar to the corymbose/digitate forms. Therefore, provide similar lighting and ensure water flow is sufficient to remove sediments. However, if a table-like or plate coral seems to be a piece broken from a much larger coral, this may indicate that the coral is from moderately deep water (about 40 meters). Theses forms require much less light and their zooxanthellae saturate at only 77 µEmS (4,235 lux of sunlight).

Arborescent (Tree-like) Forms

Arborescent forms most usually inhabit deeper and/or cálmer waters. Generally, these types of Acropora are found on reef slopes at 6 meters (19.6 feet) and below and in tranquil lagoons. The caespitose forms are found on protected reef slopes, fringing reefs and lagoons. Odds are that bottle-brush forms are lagoon corals. The branching arborescent forms live in a variety of environments and the shapes and size of the branches lend clues. Very thick, wedge shaped columns with few branches (such as A. "Isopora" palifera) are found on exposed, windward reef slopes. Their columns are thicker at the bottom to give the animal strength in this harsh environment. The radial colonies are irregular and it seems the constant water actions keep the coral from growing normally.

Most likely, the irregular shapes will reduce laminar water flow while offering a greater surface area for food capture.   The short, flattened branches depend on water movement to remove sediments.   Incidentally, this coral usually grows in to the prevailing current, that is, the largest branches are normally facing the direction from which the flow originates.   As depth increases and flow is less forceful, the branches of the arborescent types tend to become longer and more widely spaced.   The size and shape of the branches, again, lend clues as to the animal's home. Round branches are the most effective at shedding sediments.   These corals are likely to have come from slightly turbid waters, such as a lagoon or fringing reef. This type of water is common off many of the collecting spots throughout the world (Singapore, the Philippines, etc.) and is classified as a Coastal water. Type II Coastal water would describe the spectral quality. (See Chap. 3).The more turbid the water, the less light transmission; studies have shown that the angle of the branches may indicate the coral's depth and, hence, the amount of light it receives. See drawings.

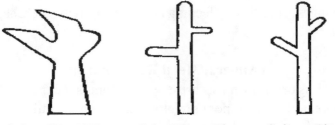

Violent Water Flow   Calm Water Flow   Calmer Flow

Light requirements vary. Acropora cervicornis saturates at about 325 µE m s. A. acuminata, in its arborescent form, saturates at about 300 µE m s.

Feeding

Scientific studies have shown Acropora corals to have a high metabolism. With enough light, zooxanthallae will supply more than enough carbon to cover respiration with the remainder fulfilling some, but not all, of the carbon required for growth and reproduction. Added to the fact that zooxanthellae will not provide a full spectrum of foods to the coral, it becomes obvious that this coral needs to eat and eat often. Further research has shown this coral to eat bacteria and zooplankton. Phytoplankton (unicellular algae) were not ingested. As with most corals, Acropora has the ability to remove dissolved organic compounds from the water. Various research papers suggest that Staghorn corals need specific proteins and fats (especially unsaturated oils) in their foods. Feeding brine shrimp is not sufficient for two reasons: 1) they do not contain all the amino acids and fatty acids needed by Acropora and 2) brine shrimp are simply too large for some Acropora polyps to ingest. For tips on feeding corals in captivity, see Chapter 31.

Mineral/Metal Requirements

It is certainly no surprise that calcium is the major component of the Acropora skeleton. Strontium is utilized vigorously in skeletal formation as well and, in fact, Acropora skeletons contain slightly more strontium than the "average" coral. Metals analyses performed on a variety of corals has shown them to contain up to 30 other metals. The exact need for these metals is presently unknown, but it does appear that some corals actively incorporate many metals, while discriminating against others.

Calcium levels should be maintained at normal levels (about 400 milligrams per liter) in the aquarium. Strontium should be added, as well. Regular water exchanges should supply various elements; some of which are essential for biological processes (such as zinc, tin, selenium and many others). A great deal of research remains to be done before the exact mineral and metal requirements are established for different coral genera.

Other Considerations

Don't be alarmed if you observe small crabs living on the branches of an Acropora colony.

These crabs, Xanthid crabs, are natural inhabitants, although there is some controversy as to whether the coral actually benefits from the relation. Xanthid crabs can be drab brown, snow white or brilliantly colored. Unless the crab is observed actually damaging the colony, it is best to leave them alone.

Xanthid Crab

The Staghorn coral (Acropora) can grow about one-half inch per month if conditions are proper.

Acropora corals are often propagated from fragments from a parent colony.

Favia corals need good lighting. It extends hundreds of tiny
tentacles when water currents are low.

The Honey Comb coral (Goniastrea) is occassionally offered
for sale.

One of the most popular stony corals, the Elegance coral (Catalaphyllia) is relatively easy to keep.

Heliofungia corals are often mistaken for sea anemones. They are delicate by nature.

The Cup or Pagoda coral (Turbinaria) will grow in a properly managed reef aquarium.

The Cactus coral (Pavona) is relatively hardy but delicately formed.

The Open Brain coral (Trachyphyllia) can live for years if properly cared for. Green or red varieties are often seen.

The Finger coral (Hydnophora) needs good lighting and strong water flow. It is an aggressive coral.

The Mushroom coral is a good candidate for the beginning hobbyist. It can actually "walk" away from a spot it dislikes.

The Anchor coral (Euphyllia) gets its name from it tentacle's shape. It is not difficult to maintain.

The Sun coral (Tubastraea) belies its name as it prefers dim lighting. It is demanding in its feeding requirements.

Goniopora, or the FlowerPot coral, is quite distinctive. It can be recommended to the advanced hobbyist.

The Bubble coral (Plerogyra) is a popular addition to the reef aquarium. It will thrive with proper care.

These Actinodiscus are false corals. They come in many colors.

The soft corals Xenia, actually pulsate when conditions are proper.

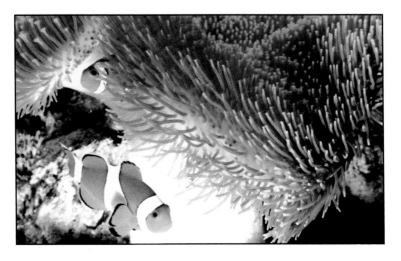

Two clown fish play around a leather coral, Sarcophyton.

The Star polyps, Clavularia, is a desireable aquarium inhabitant.

Lobophytum is commonly available and can be recommended to the beginning hobbyist.

Sinularia comes in many shapes. This is the arborescent, or tree-like, form.

The soft coral, Tubipora, builds a brick-red skeleton that resembles an organ pipe.

The Captive Reef

Chapter 18

The Elegance Corals
CATALAPHYLLIA

Pronounced Ca-tal-ah-fill-ee-ah

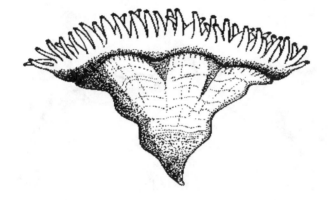

One of the most notable stony corals available is the Elegance or Elegans coral. Its large polyp body is striped green and brown; hundreds of white tentacles are tipped with purple, pink or red spheres. The striking appearance is often matched with a striking price. Fortunately, the Elegance coral is relatively easy to maintain in captivity and can therefore be recommended as a "beginner's" stony coral.

Where Do Catalaphyllia Corals Live in Nature?

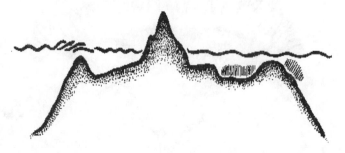

Catalaphyllia prefers turbid waters, such as back reefs and lagoon slopes. It is often found at depths of 8 to 10 meters (about 25 to 30 feet) with its cone shaped skeleton buried in soft substate. It is believed that Catalaphyllia's skeleton stabilizes the sediments and, after the coral dies, the skeleton acts as a platform for new coral growths.

Water Currents

That the Elegance coral lives on a soft bottom indicates that currents are not sufficient to maintain particles in suspension. This coral's high polyp-to-skeleton ratio gives it an excellent ability to shed sediments.

We can therefore expect the water current to be just a few centimeters per second.

Lighting Requirements

The minimum amount of light for this coral seems to be about 150 μE m s. This amount of radiation can be supplied by four 110-watt VHO fluorescents (in a "reef" bulb/actinic combination) or 2-175 watt metal halide bulbs. From a purely aesthetic point of view, a combination of metal halides and actinic bulbs will make this coral "glow" (while supplying enough light). Incidentally, it is a common mistake to believe that Catalaphyllia's brilliant green coloration is due to its symbiotic algae. It is not. The color is due to substances (proteins) that act as a protective sun screen. Any brown coloration is due to the zooxanthellae.

Feeding

Catalaphyllia apparently derives most of its nutrition from its symbiotic algae. It is likely that this coral also eats bacteria and absorbs dissolved organic and inorganic substances (including calcium and strontium). Recent experiments have shown that feeding responses are triggered by the amino acids glycine, lysine and taurine. Feeding any food of ocean-origin (such as shrimp, oysters, fish, etc.) seems to satisfy this coral's nutritional requirements.

Chapter 19

The
Anchor, Hammer and Frogspawn Corals
EUPHYLLIA
Pronounced You-fill-ee-ah

Euphyllia species are rather common in pet shops with the Anchor coral (E. ancora) and the Octopus coral (E. divisa) being the most common.

Where Do Euphyllia Corals Live in Nature?

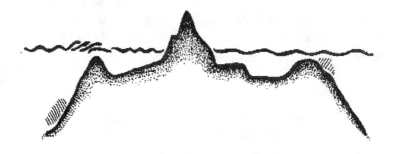

There are over a dozen Euphyllia species and these inhabit a wide range of habitats. Some species inhabit protected, turbid reef flats; others, such as E. ancora, may be the dominant species in deep water.

Water Currents

As with many corals from sheltered sites, Euphyllia enjoys a moderate water flow. Perhaps the best indicator of appropriate flow is the appearance of this coral's sweeper tentacles. With proper currents, these defense tentacles may stretch 7 inches or 8 inches past the smaller tentacles. If the coral is healthy and is expanding, try increasing the flow across it and watch for the sweepers.

Lighting Requirements

Euphyllia is most abundant in nature when light levels are 100 - 600 μE m s.   Although just two 110-watt VHO bulbs will supply the bare minimum lighting, 4-VHO tubes is a better choice as is two 175-watt metal halides.   Of course, a combination of metal halides and fluorecents will allow a dawn and dusk effect if the lights are on separate timers. This combination will allow Euphyllia to be placed in any part of the aquarium and receive sufficient light.

Feeding

Euphyllia naturally feeds upon large zooplankton, flesh fragments and small fishes.   Feed this coral once or twice a week with a variety of appropriate foods. All food should originate from the oceans. Feeder guppies and goldfish do not contain many marine oils and fatty acids.   Pet stores often offer frozen fishes such as silversides. Larger groceries usually have fresh sea foods, as well.

Be certain to monitor and maintain calcium levels of around 500 ppm.   Strontium addition is also important as the Euphyllia skeleton is usually about 1% strontium by weight.

Chapter 20

The Star Corals
FAVIA
Pronounced Fay-vee-ah

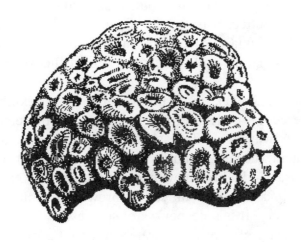

Favia, or the Star coral, is a favorite subject of re-searchers. Found in both the Atlantic and Pacific Oceans, it would seem that they would be more common in reef aquaria. They are only occasionally offered for sale. They are generally hardy and can regrow tissue lost to small injuries such as bristleworm feedings.

With about 70 species listed, it is possible to discuss only a few. At first glance, Favia appears to be similar to the Honeycomb coral (Goniastrea) and Favites. With a little practice, it is easy to distinguish between these animals. Favia's polyps have individual coralla and are clearly separate with a distinct groove between each polyp.

Favia comes in many colors; those exhibiting fluorescence under actinic lights are from relatively shallow waters. Two shallow water Favias are F. stelligera (usually a uniform green or brown) and F. speciosa (light brown with different colored calices). F. maxima is brown or yellow-brown with dull green oral disks. It is a deeper water species.

Favia prefers warmer waters of about 25°C.

Water Currents

Small, flattened Favia should receive water currents strong enough to flush away accumulated detritus. While dome-shaped specimens shed sediments without the aid of currents, they still enjoy moderate water flow, as well. Current generating devices should be turned off when the animal feeds, which is usually at night.

Where Do Favia Corals Live in Nature?

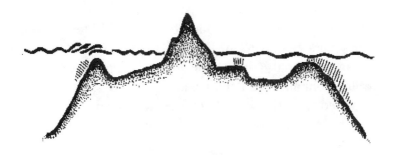

Lighting Requirements

If your Favia exhibits the shallow water trait of fluorescence under actinic lighting, absolute minimal lighting would be two 110-watt VHO "reef" bulbs. This set-up allows no room for error - the lighting system must be as close to the water surface as possible and must be replaced every few months. A "reef" bulb and actinic combination would be a better choice. At these light levels, the coral will live, but will not thrive. Two 175-watt metal halides supplemented with actinics or four 110-watt VHO's offer acceptable amounts of radiation. Deeper water Favias (such as F. maxima) still need metal halides or VHO fluorecents to even begin to approach the amount of light they get in nature.

Feeding Favia

Aside from the foods translocated from the coral's zoox-anthellae, Favia feeds on zooplankton and flesh fragments. An active night feeder, scientists have determined that Favia "filters" seawater for food at about 80 milliliters per hour per square centimeter of living tissue. Favia also uptakes organic materials (such as the amino acid, glycine) from the water column. Calcium and strontium should also be supplied as it is needed for skeleton formation. Favia skeletons contain above average amounts of strontium.

Chapter 21

The Mushroom Corals
FUNGIA
Pronounced Fun-gee-ah

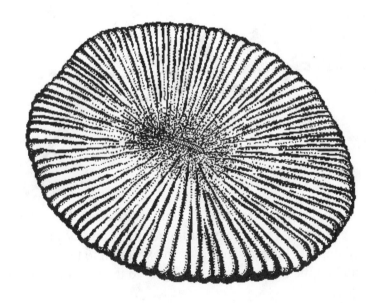

Fungia is not likely to be confused with any other coral. Its distinctive flattened or slightly domed disk-shaped body has given it the popular name of Mushroom coral. It is no wonder that these corals are common in dealer's tanks; Fungia lives unattached to the ocean bottom - collectors just scoop them up!

Where Do Fungia Corals Live in Nature?

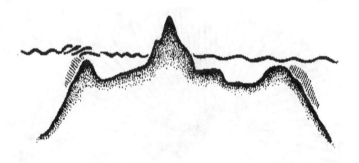

Fungia prefers relatively calm waters away from strong wave action. They are often found in lagoons or protected reef slopes. Fungia scutaria is an exception to the rule: it is found on the reef crest and is subject to the pounding of the surf.

Water Currents

Close observation by the aquarist will determine the best placement for Fungia in the aquarium. By necessity, it must be placed on the aquarium bottom. Water flow must bathe the animal and at the same time, not be too strong. Fungia's feeding strategies include covering itself with a mucus "net." Too much flow will wash the mucus and the entrapped food away. Air bubbles can also lift the net away.

Lighting Requirements

Fungia's natural environment subjects it to 2% to 30% of surface irradiance, which equates to roughly 40 to 600 μE m s. Common 40-watt bulbs (actinic and "reef" bulb combo) will produce the bare minimum of light required for this coral's survival. Should the aquarist choose to use these lights, carefully observe the animal every morning for its mucus net. Should this be routinely visible, we know that the coral is getting enough light (mucus production is light dependent). If the mucus production does not appear, reduce water flow. If mucus is not visible in the next day or two, or if mucus production has stopped, increase the amount of lighting. Acclimate the animal slowly to the new light regime; full acclimation will take about a month. Obtaining just 30% of surface irradiance in an aquarium is quite a feat and is usually not practical. Metal halides and VHO actinics will likely be required to satisfy this animal's needs.

Feeding Fungia

Under the best of conditions, zooxanthellae will supply about 70% of Fungia's daily carbon requirements. Food is needed to supply the remaining 30% and that carbon required for growth or reproduction. Fungia is an avid feeder.

It reportedly eats jellyfish in nature. Under suitable conditions, Fungia produces mucus that enters the food web. Bacterioplankton eat the mucus and Fungia eats the bacterioplankton. The mucus also captures various organic substances of animal and bacterial origin. Cilia will move the mucus net and the entrapped particles to the coral's mouth for ingestion. Fungia has also been found to absorb dissolved substances from the water column, including the amino acids tyrosine, lysine, aspartic acid and glycine, as well as lactate and phosphorus. It is interesting that aspartic acid is obtained in this manner, as this amino acid is critical in skeletogenesis. That Fungia absorbs it from the water suggests the coral does not make this critical substance or needs a supplemental source to that produced by zooxanthellae or gastrovascular flora. The amino acid proline triggers a feeding response. Scientists have measured Fungia's metabolism and have found it to be only moderate.

This animal also needs calcium, strontium and a variety of trace elements in order to produce a skeleton.

Other Considerations

Optimum temperature for this coral is 26°C. When purchasing Fungia, carefully inspect its stony underside for the wentletrap snail, Epitonium or its eggs (see Chapter 32). Fungia is able to "walk" and can move significant distances (inches, if not feet) overnight. It is likely to fall from rocky supports or ledges and injure itself. It should be placed on the aquarium's bottom. Consider this closely as light levels drop rapidly in even shallow aquaria.

Chapter 22

The Honeycomb Corals
GONIASTREA

Pronounced Gon-ee-ass-tree-ah

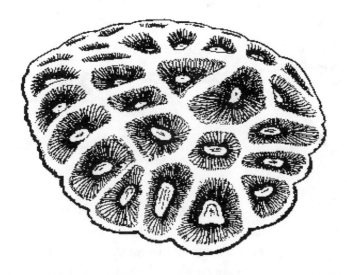

Perhaps Goniastrea's popular name should be changed. Not that the nickname isn't appropriate; its coralla share a common wall and it does indeed resemble a 4 or 6 sided honeycomb. However, the "Bullet-proof" coral would also be an appropriate moniker.

There is believed to be as many as 35 species in this genus.

Where Do Goniastrea Specimens Live in Nature?

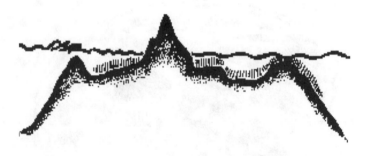

Goniastrea lives where no other coral can. They take the full force of waves or live on reef flats where high sedimentation rates, emergence during low tide, and high or low temperatures and salinities would kill other corals. Specimens offered for sale are often (and understandably) stunted in growth. Goniastrea is often the dominant coral on reef flats covered by just 1 or 2 meters of water. The average temperature experienced by this coral is about 26° C.

Water Currents

Goniastrea appreciates good water movement as it is subjected to almost constantly changing tides in nature. Wave making devices that alternate powerheads may be appropriate here. Reduce flow if small tentacles are not observed at night.

Feeding Goniastrea

Studies have shown that zooxanthellae will produce 100% of this coral's daily carbon requirements. If the coral is to grow or reproduce, additional carbon and other nutritive substances will be needed. Goniastrea is a predatory coral and should be fed the smallest scraps of shrimp or squid (for protein), oysters (for carbohydrates) and ground whole krill for fats and oils. This is crucial in low light situations (which is the case in the vast majority of reef tanks). This animal also feeds on bacteria and dissolved organic matter.

For skeleton growth, supply strontium on a regular basis as well as kalkwasser for calcium.

Lighting Requirements

Since Goniastrea is a shallow water coral, it often receives a great deal of light. Estimates of 30% to 90% of surface irradiance is considered the norm. The maximum amount of light received by this animal is a staggering 1,780 μE m s. This is well beyond what any average aquarium lighting system can produce. This is not to say that Goniastrea cannot be maintained.

Metal halides (in the 250-watt configuration, or better) combined with VHO actinics may produce light pulses (with proper water surface motion) to saturate this coral's zooxanthellae. Is the animal producing mucus? This is a good sign that lighting is powering the symbiotic algae and producing lipids. Corals can live in less than optimum lighting conditions but may never thrive.

If one is sure that a Goniastrea specimen has not lost its coloration during shipping or holding, it may be possible to tell the approximate depth from which the animal was collected. Shallow water specimens are colored cream, pink, green or pale brown and will fluoresce under actinic lighting. Deeper water corals are darker pink or brown.

Goniastrea will repair small injuries in a well maintained aquarium.

Chapter 23

The Flower Pot Corals
GONIOPORA
Pronounced Gon-ee-oh-pore-ah

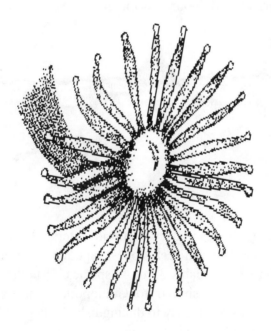

Healthy Goniopora corals are quite unique in appearance and are easy to identify. When fully expanded, their hundreds of stalks and thousands of tentacles do indeed resemble a pot full of flowers. These corals have a reputation as being difficult to maintain in captivity. If we cater to their needs, they can live for years in a well maintained reef aquarium.

Where Do Goniopora Specimens Live in Nature?

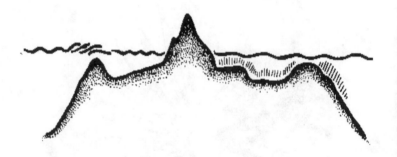

Goniopora thrives in deep or turbid waters. They are often found on sheltered reef slopes, lagoons or turbid reef flats. There are probably 35 or 40 species. Another coral, Alveopora, is very similar to Goniopora in appearance. The two are, however, easy to distinguish: Alveopora has 12 tentacles per stalk; Goniopora has 24.

Water Currents

Since Goniopora is found in turbid waters with soft substrates and is known for its sediment shedding ability, we can expect the water currents it would experience to be quite low. Periods of moderate flow, however, (enough to bend but not kink the tentacles) seems to be appreciated. Feed Goniopora during times of low flow. Lagoon currents are estimated to be 2 to 45 centimeters (about 1 to 18 inches) per second. Don't "beat" this coral with excessive flow or it will fail to expand. If it can't expand, its zooxanthellae aren't exposed to light and, therefore, cannot photosynthesize.

Feeding Goniopora

Goniopora is a fast-growing coral in nature; it has to be or it would be buried by sediments. Its zooxanthellae seem to play an important part in supplying some of the nutrition required for rapid growth. It has been estimated that, under ideal conditions, the zooxanthellae will supply 120% of the animal's daily carbon requirement. The remaining 20% goes towards, but will not satisfy, the carbon required for growth and reproduction. Therefore, Goniopora must eat in order to thrive. It is a predatory coral that feeds on zooplankton. Recent research has shown a variety of amino acids, including ornithine, taurine, cysteine, glycine, lysine and phenylalanine trigger a feeding response. It is likely that these can be absorbed from the water column along with other organic nutrients, such as fatty acids. It is interesting to note that Goniopora contains more fats in its tissues than most other stony corals.

It is possible that Goniopora needs a high fat diet.   It may also indicate that its metabolism prefers to "burn" carbohydrates and proteins preferentially.

Bacteria may also be a source of nutrition to this coral. Researchers have found the Goniopora skeleton to contain above average amounts of strontium and normal amounts of calcium.

Lighting Requirements

Sufficient lighting must be maintained in order for the zooxanthellae to function properly.   Goniopora are abundant in areas receiving 100 to 600 μE m s.   Two 175-watt metal halides and two VHO actinic tubes will supply an adequate amount of light.   Two 250 watt metal halides with supplemental actinics is even better.

Additional Comments

Goniopora is apparently susceptible to bacterial infections.   Any tissue damage, whether caused by a fall, or otherwise, is to be avoided.   Overgrowth by Caulerpa algae is also detrimental.   Should damage occur, it is important to promptly treat the infection.   I have had good success with erythomycin at 200 mg/l for 24 hours in a bare hospital tank.

Some Goniopora react negatively (and almost immediately) when the aquarist places his bare hands in the aquarium.   Wearing latex surgical gloves when working in the aquarium will prevent this reaction.

Chapter 24

The Plate Corals
HELIOFUNGIA

Pronounced Heel-ee-oh-fun-gee-ah

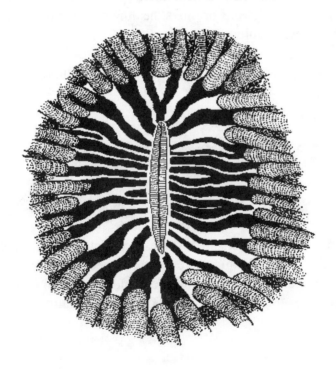

Heliofungia is remarkably similar to Fungia. Heliofungia's long anemone-like tentacles are the major difference. Heliofungia, like Goniopora and Acropora, has a reputation as being difficult to maintain in captivity. There is only one species, Heliofungia actiniformis. This coral's tentacles are usually beige colored with white bulbous tips. It is the oral disk that makes this coral so attractive. Often striped with alternating zebra-like patterns of fluorescent greens or pinks, healthy specimens are magnificent when fully expanded.

Where Does Heliofungia Live in Nature?

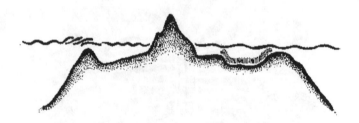

Found on protected reef slopes, reef flats and patch reefs, along with Fungia, we can expect Heliofungia's requirements for water movement and lighting to be about the same. See the Fungia section for full details.

Feeding Heliofungia

Strong lighting will cause zooxanthellae to "produce" enough carbon daily to satisfy Heliofungia's respiration requirements. For growth and reproduction, the coral will gain nutriment from predatory feeding, bacteria and dissolved organic materials. Heliofungia's body tissues are about 50% protein, 30% to 35% fat with the remainder being carbohydrates or the inorganic substances called ash. Interestingly, its tissues contain a relatively large amount of sugar, which is likely translocated from the zooxanthellae.

Additional Comments

If Heliofungia doesn't like its location, it will take a hike - literally. Unfortunately, this excursion will result in the coral's death if it falls off a ledge. The fall doesn't kill it; the resulting bacterial infection will, if not treated. For those wishing to save an injured coral, experimentation with erythomycin or streptomycin might - repeat, might - do the trick.

Chapter 25

The Finger Corals
HYDNOPHORA
Pronounced Hide-no-fore-ah

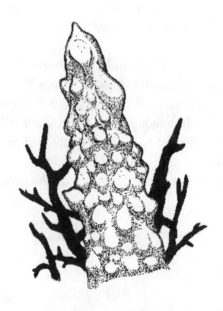

Hydnophora is infrequently offered for sale. It is so uncommon that it does not have a popular name. It can be a spectacular coral, resembling a green, "bumpy" Acropora. (It is these "bumps," called hydnopores, that gives this coral its name). Hydnophora is generally sold in its tree-like or arborescent form. There are about 20 species, and come in different shapes: massive, encrusting and the previously mentioned arborescent form.

Where Do Hydnophora Specimens Live in Nature?

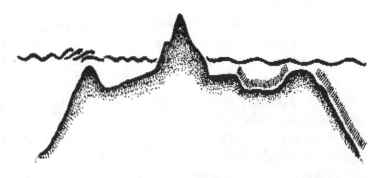

Hydnophora generally lives in lagoons, reef slopes or other protected sites. It prefers a temperature of about 26° C.

Water Currents

Being a lagoon or sheltered slope coral, Hydnophora will not require a great deal of current. Powerheads can produce enough flow to satisfy this animal. Watch polyp expansion and small mesenterial filaments. These should not be "flapping in the breeze."

Lighting Requirements

A minimum of 300 µE m s seems to be required by this coral.   Two 175-watt metal halides and two 110-watt VHO bulbs suspended about 4 inches over the surface of a 4- foot reef tank should be sufficient to produce the required radiation.   Of course, VHO fluorescents can be used if enough of them can be stuffed above the tank.

Feeding Hydnophora

This coral's polyps are relatively large, but the mouths are quite tiny.   Even newly hatched brine shrimp are likely to be too large.   Feeding rotifers may be an option for the dedicated aquarist.   As with most corals, Hydnophora eats the tiniest of zooplankton, bacteria, protozoa and flesh fragments.   It most likely gets fatty acids, vitamins and amino acids from the water column, as well.

A varied diet of clam, oyster and shrimp that have been liquefied in a blender may be sufficient.   For good measure, add a drop or two of vitamins.   Various feeding methods are discussed in greater detail in the chapter on feeding.   Calcium and strontium should, of course, be added to the reef tank.

One last note - all corals have a rather distinctive odor. Hydnophora is the odor champion with a smell something like a mix of burning electrical wire and hydrogen sulfide gas.

Chapter 26

The Cactus Corals
PAVONA

Pronounced Pa-vo-na

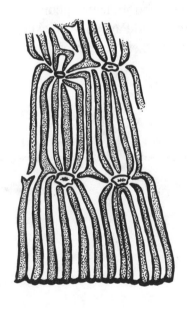

The Pavona corals are included here for special reasons. Coral researchers have theorized that Pavona is probably as close as possible to being a fully autotrophic animal. That is, the zooxanthellae produce most of the coral's carbon requirements for respiration, growth and reproduction. Some Pavona species (there are about 50) are foliaceous, or leaf-like, with a high surface-to-volume ratio. In addition, it has small polyps. All this indicates Pavona is specialized for capturing light and indicates phototrophy. In addition, researchers have found Pavona to be exceptionally hardy, as this coral suffered zero fatalities during transplantation experiments.

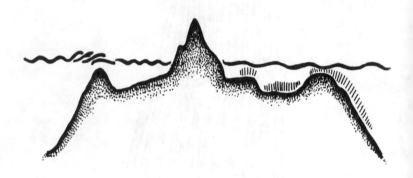

Where Do Pavona Corals Live in Nature?

The Cactus coral prefers shallow, protected waters such as lagoons, sheltered reef slopes and fringing reefs. All these areas are generally considered to be turbid. Optimal growth temperature for this coral has been found to be 24°C to 25°C.

Water Currents

Pavona, coming from sheltered waters, enjoys a moderate water flow. An easy way to tell if the coral is getting sufficient flow is to closely study the coral for its defense mechanisms, the sweeper tentacles. They may not be easy to see as they are usually unpigmented (white or clear), hair-like and less than an inch long. These should wave gently in the currents and be extended more or less horizontally. Currents of just a few centimeters per second should be adequate.

Feeding

Scientists tell us that, under ideal conditions, the zooxanthellae will provide enough carbon to cover this animal's daily maintenance and growth. The amount required for reproduction is almost entirely covered also. If the coral could live alone on the carbon materials synthesized, then it probably would not need to eat. It, like all living creatures, needs a variety of elements and compounds in order to survive. Since its polyps are so tiny, it eats protozoa, such as ciliates, single-celled algae (unusual for a coral) and bacteria. Calcium and strontium additions are a must for skeleton growth.

Lighting Requirements

Obviously, Pavona needs enough light to saturate its zooxanthellae.   In nature, it is most abundant in areas receiving 160 to 1,340 µE m s.   After acclimating this coral to the aquarium, it is best to place it where it will receive maximum illumination.   It is doubtful that Pavona can be over-illuminated (it would take 12 new 110-watt VHO fluorescents over a four foot tank to equal the amount of light Pavona naturally gets).   I have used 250-watt metal halides with supplemental VHO actinics with good success.

Other Considerations

Pavona is a rather delicate coral.   Since it should be placed near the water's surface in order to get maximum il-lumination, this means it will probably be perched atop the live rock.   Any fall will break it.   Unlike some corals, Pavona does not seem prone to bacterial infections, so it will likely survive the fall and recover from its injuries.

It should go without saying that the aquarist should take measures to prevent the animal from taking a tumble.   Un-fortunately, there is usually little exposed skeleton to use as a contact point for epoxy.   Perhaps the best answer is to fit one of Pavona's "leaves" into a live rock crevice.

Chapter 27

The Bubble Corals
PLEROGYRA
Pronounced Plero-jai-rah

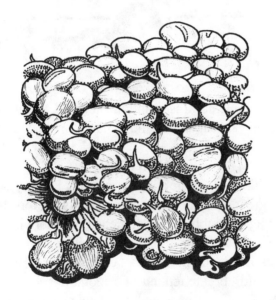

A reef aquarium can be quite dramatic when it contains a healthy, fully expanded Bubble coral.   Show specimens are often available at reasonable prices.   In addition, these corals are noted to be very hardy.   There are probably 6 species.

Where Do Plerogyra Specimens Live in Nature?

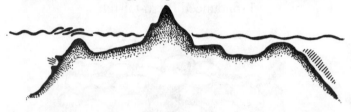

The Bubble coral is found in sheltered, turbid waters, protected vertical slopes and in caves or shaded crevices.

Water Flow

As with many of the aquarium corals, Plerogyra does not need a great deal of current.   If currents are too strong, the rather fragile "bubbles" are flattened or otherwise distorted and the coral may not fully expand.   The animal's sweeper tentacles are a good indicator of correct flow.   These sweepers should be extended horizontally by the flow. Incidentally, these tentacles can extend about as much as the coral's body width.   In other words, a Bubble coral 8 inches across (when fully expanded) can possess sweepers 8 inches long (in the case of Plerogyra sinuosa).

Feeding Plerogyra

Plerogyra seems to be mostly predatory by nature and

doesn't present any unusual challenges in feeding. Its large, single mouth accepts relatively large chunks of food. A varied diet of fish, oysters, shrimp and squid seems to be sufficient. The Bubble coral will likely absorb dissolved organic compounds, as well. Obvious mucus nets do not seem to be used for food capture.

Lighting

Plerogyra is most often found at levels where the percentage of surface irradiance is 5% to 39%. Four 40 watt fluorescents (2 actinics and 2 daylights) will produce enough PAR at the low end for Bubble corals. However, this leaves no room for error and two VHO bulbs of 110 watts each or two 175-watt metal halides allows for bulb and luminaire depreciation.

Other Considerations

Plerogyra demands good water quality. Even with a good protein skimmer and rigorous maintenance techniques, this coral "perks up" after a water exchange.

If placed too close to a dominate coral (such as Euphyllia), Plerogyra can develop an allergy to its neighbor and not expand fully.

As with all corals, Plerogyra can be badly damaged by falls, so the wise aquarist should take steps to prevent such occurrences. A good grade marine epoxy (made for underwater use) will secure specimens to a live rock base.

Plerogyra's sting is reported to pack a wallop. It is not a bad idea to wear surgical gloves when handling or working around this animal.

Chapter 28

The Open Brain Corals
TRACHYPHYLLIA
Pronounced Trak-ee-fill-ee-ah

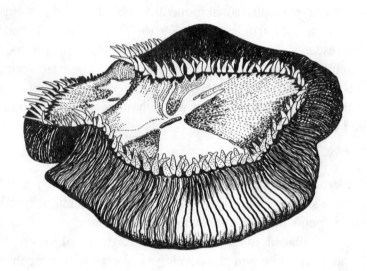

Trachyphyllia is an excellent choice for the beginning reef hobbyist. This coral is very hardy, in fact, it can be critically injured and, with proper care, recover. It is not particularly demanding in its lighting requirements. Its varied colors (ranging from fluorescent green to fluorescent orange-red) make it a welcome addition to any hobbyist's tank. There is believed to be 6 species.

Where Do Trachyphyllia Specimens Live in Nature?

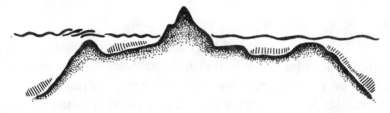

Trachyphyllia prefers turbid waters near continental islands or deeper clear protected waters. It is also found in lagoons. The Open Brain coral is sometimes common on exposed lower reef slopes, but at depths where wave action is minimal.

Water Currents

As long as water movement does not blast this animal, it does not seem very concerned about currents. Its high polyp-to-skeleton ratio indicates that it is an excellent sediment shedder, which is a further indication that the currents it experiences in nature are not sufficient to maintain particles in suspension. It most likely buries its cone shaped skeleton in soft substrates.

Lighting Requirements

Trachyphyllia enjoys irradiance at about 5% to 30% of that at the surface. This is equivalent to 100 to 600 µE m s. The combination of two 40-watt actinic and two 40-watt daylight fluorescent lights, along with supplemental sunlight, will meet this animal's minimum light needs. However, two 175-watt metal halides with two 40-watt actinic fluorescents or perhaps two to three 110-watt VHO fluorescents would be a better choice.

Feeding Trachyphyllia

This coral is quite able to ingest larger fish, shrimp or oyster flesh fragments. It also "casts" small mucus nets to capture invisible protozoa and bacteria. Its hundreds of tentacles are well armed with thousands of nematocysts or stinging cells with which it captures larger prey, such as newly hatched brine shrimp. When fed, this animal quickly senses the food and will rapidly fold part of its body to push the food particle to one of its many mouths. Apparently the coral swallows a great deal of water when ingesting larger food particles as its body rapidly swells immediately after feeding. Of course, zooxanthellae will provide a major portion of the animal's food.

Calcium is the major component of the coral's skeleton. The hobbist shoud take measures to provide this element.

Chapter 29

The Sun Corals
TUBASTRAEA
Pronounced Tube-ass-tree-ah

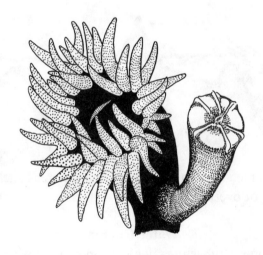

Tubastrea is perhaps the perfect stony coral for the beginning reef hobbyist. Its bright orange coloration and beautiful polyps make it an eye-catching center piece. Its only demands are regular feedings and above average water currents. If the aquarist is conscientious in meeting this animals requirements, Tubastraea might reward those efforts by spawning.

Where Do Tubastrea Specimens Live in Nature?

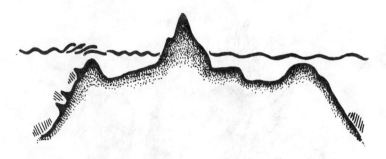

Tubastraea lives in caves or in shaded areas such as crevices or overhangs.

Water Currents

In nature, Tubastraea depends upon good water currents to bring it food. The aquarium's water circulation pump(s) should be turned off when feeding the coral. Good flow will be needed to carry away waste products. A small powerhead aimed indirectly at this animal should provide enough circulation. If the coral never expands, reduce the flow and monitor it for a couple of days. Make flow adjustments as needed.

Feeding

Tubastraea's tentacles have nematocysts for capturing foods. It is noted as a ravenous predator. It is known to feed on protozoa (ciliates in particular) as well as larger zooplankton and even small fishes. Researchers have found the Sun coral to uptake from solution the amino acid leucine, which is an important component of the animal's organic matrix. None of Tubastraea's natural food sources can be found to occur insufficient numbers in the aquarium; the coral should be fed daily.

The Tubastraea skeleton is composed of mostly calcium with an above average strontium content. Take appropriate steps to supply these important elements.

Lighting Requirements

Since this animal contains no zooxanthellae, lighting is largely a matter of preference on the hobbyist's part.

Other Considerations

Should Tubastraea planulate (spawn) in the aquarium, see the chapter on Reproduction.

Chapter 30

The Cup Corals
TURBINARIA

Pronounced Tur-by-nair-ee-ah

The Cup coral (Turbinaria) is an attractive and relatively easy-to-maintain resident of the captive reef.   With almost 80 species, only generalizations about its care can be made.

Where Do Turbinaria Specimens Live in Nature?

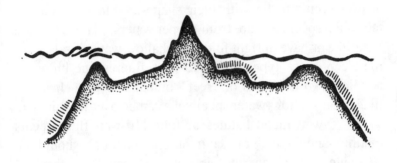

Some species prefer reef slopes, while others prefer shallow turbid water.   Generally, the Cup coral is found in waters averaging about 23° C.

Water Currents

This coral seems perfectly content with little water flow. However, occasional current strong enough to wash away any sediments that have collected in the "cup" will be appreciated.   If currents cannot be provided, then the detritus should be gently removed with a baster or similar device.

Lighting Requirements

Different Turbinaria species have different light requirements, but studies have shown these animals are most often
found at depths receiving 2% to 39% surface irradiance. In
microEinsteins, this equates to 40 to 780. How do we know
if the coral is a shallow- or deep-water specimen? The
answer seems to lie with their shapes. Flattened cup or
table-like specimens are from deeper waters. Those that are
vase-like or have upright folds are shallow water corals. For
the deep-water types, four 40-watt fluorescent bulbs (2
actinics, two daylights or "reef" bulbs) will do. It is not
likely that shallow-water specimens can be over illuminated.
Two 175-watt metal halides or four 110-watt fluorescents
(actinic and "reef" or daylight combination) should be
adequate if the aquarium is not too deep (less than 18
inches).

Feeding Turbinaria

Close observation of the Cup coral will reveal (if the water
current is not too strong) a whipping action among a few of its
many tentacles. Apparently it is capturing microscopic zooplankton. Turbinaria is not difficult to feed if the foods
(fish,oysters, squid, etc.) have been liquefied in a blender.
Turbinaria will grow in the aquarium if fed and calcium and
strontium are supplied regularly.

Chapter 31

FEEDING YOUR CORALS

Corals, like other living things, need a proper diet in order to survive. It is true that the zooxanthellae can provide enough carbon to cover the daily requirements of many corals.

Researchers believe the relationship between the symbiotic algae and one species of Xenia has evolved to the point where the animal's digestive system is practically useless; therefore it relies on its internal algae to provide food. This relationship is called autotrophic. On the other hand, corals such as Tubastraea (the Orange or Sun coral), contain no zooxanthellae and must eat zooplankton in order to survive. Tubastraea is said to be heterotrophic. Somewhere in between lie the majority of corals; those that receive some nutrition from the zooxanthellae, but must continue to eat in order to have a balanced diet. Different species of corals are likely to have differing nutritional needs. Some corals may use one or more feeding strategies. To understand what corals need to eat, we must first understand what they are made of.

What Is A Coral Made Of?

Corals are composed of two major factions: the skeleton and the soft tissues.   These will be dealt with separately. First the soft tissues.   The "fleshy" portion of the coral is made of four elements: proteins, lipids (fats), carbohydrates and ash.   Table 9 details the average percentages of these components.

Table 9
Proteins/carbohydrates: 54%
Lipids: 32%
Ash: 14%

Proteins

Proteins (from the Greek word "proteios," meaning first or primary) composes a major portion of a corals dry tissue weight, just as it does in most living creatures.   Proteins are essential for life, as they act as structural tissues, enzymes, hormones, digestive secretions, etc.   Proteins are composed of building blocks called amino acids.   All amino acids contain carbon, hydrogen, nitrogen and oxygen.   Some additionally contain sulphur, phosphorus, iron, zinc and copper. Two amino acids are known to be essential in the calcification process: glutamic acid and aspartic acid.   The amino acid content of corals will differ from species to species.   It is important to note that nitrogen, in the form of proteins, is the limiting element in coral growth.   I will repeat: nitrogen is the limiting element in coral growth!

Nitrogen, in the forms of ammonia or nitrate may be used for growth by the symbiotic algae and they supply the coral with various nitrogen containing compounds, the coral will need nitrogen in the form of proteins. The amino acid requirements, like the amino acid content, will likely vary between species.

Table 10 details a comparison of the amino acid content of two Mushroom corals.

Table 10		
A Comparison of the Organic Matrix Amino Acid Content of Two Mushroom Coral Species		
	Fungia scutaria	Fungia echinata
Amino Acid	Occurrences per 1000 units	
Aspartic Acid	201	115
Glycine	126	134
Glutamic Acid	114	118
Serine	100	88
Threonine	77	42
Alanine	73	94
Leucine	73	115
Proline	69	71
Valine	63	69
Ilenine	44	49
Phenylalanine	41	64
Tyrosine	12	30
Methionine	6	12
Ornithine/ Histidine	0	0
Lysine/Arginine	Present	Present

Amino acids are important feeding activators as well; i.e., the coral "smells" an amino acid that triggers a feeding response. Different amino acids cause different corals to feed and this may indicate differing nutritional requirements.

Lipids

Lipids are fats or oils. Lipids usually compose 25% to 35% of coral dry tissue weight. Researchers believe this tells us two things. First, when the fat content exceeds 5% of body weight it is usually considered to be an energy reserve. Second, lipids can indicate how often an animal needs to be fed. When lipid levels are low (about 10%), the animal probably needs constant feeding. In the case of corals, it seems that often, but not constant, feeding is required. On average, 90% of lipids are contained in the coral animal. The other 10% is found in the symbiotic zooxanthellae. Fatty acids can vary dramatically just as proteins do. For instance, the Flower Pot coral (Goniopora) contains almost 35 times the amount of lipid found in the massive coral Favia. In coral tissues, the most important fatty acid is Palmitic acid, a saturated fat (16:0). Apparently, zooxanthellae can supply this fatty acid along with 16:1 (an unsaturated FA called Palmitoleic), 18:0 (a saturated fat called Stearic) and 18:1 (Oleic acid which is unsaturated). Other fatty acids found in corals include: 12:0, 14:0, 18:2, 18:3, 18:4, 18:5, 20:U (unsaturated FA's), 20:0, 22:U(unsaturated) and 22:0.

Lipids have been found to rise and fall proportionally with light levels. Since many corals spawn in the spring when internal fat and oil levels are being increased as a result of zooxanthellae being stimulated by increasing light, we could assume that lipids play an important part in coral reproduction. Coral eggs and planula often contain relatively large amounts of fats and oils as an energy reserve.

Ash

The inorganic residue (that which will not burn) is called ash. In corals, ash is considerable, at about 14%, and is likely composed of metals and salts ranging from aluminum to zinc. Major components are likely to be those elements being concentrated for skeletal growth, such as: barium, calcium, magnesium, manganese, strontium and sodium. We can also expect to find iron, copper, zinc, aluminum, iodine, selenium, cobalt and at least 13 other elements.

Carbohydrates

The exact average carbohydrate content of coral tissue is not known, but the percentage is likely to be low. Zooxanthellae supply carbohydrates in the form of glycerol (an alcohol) and glucose (a sugar). It is believed that carbohydrates are used immediately as a food source or may be incorporated into lipids and stored.

Now that we have a fair idea of what a coral is made of, we will focus on the strategies used to obtain nutrition.

Feeding Strategies

To obtain food, corals both eat and drink. They eat many things. Bacteria, detritus, zooplankton, phytoplankton (rarely and then in tiny amounts), protozoa, worms, shrimps, jellyfish, fishes and more have been listed as coral foods. The methods employed to capture the foods are almost as varied as the foods themselves.

The Mucus Net

When exposed to enough light, the coral and its internal algae produce large amounts of fixed carbon that must be shed. It is usually in the form of mucus, which contains protein, fats, etc. The coral excretes mucus and its body is covered with a thin layer.

As disgusting as this sounds, mucus is great food. Bacteria love to eat mucus. Protozoa (such as ciliates) love to eat bacteria. Corals love to eat bacteria and protozoa. Now this mucus is some pretty sticky stuff. Some of the bacteria and protozoa get stuck in it. Any other small particles touching the stuff might get caught, too. Detritus (which is usually organic in nature, hence its common name, "organic snow") particles are sometimes captured. Bacteria and protozoa eat the detritus too, so a detrital particle delivers its content and small life forms as a food. Bacteria might not seem like much of a food but consider that they contain at least 30 elements, such as: nitrogen, phosphorus (both good in this case), iron, copper, zinc, molybdenum, cobalt, etc. Likewise for protozoa. It's easy to see that lots of stuff gets caught in the mucus net. Portions of the mucus net are moved to the mouth(s) for ingestion by small whip-like appendages called cilia. Mucus not ingested will be cast off and become part of the marine food web.

Drinking for Food

This feeding strategy should be pretty familiar. Some humans drink milk as a food. But we drink milk through our mouth. The coral can do this, but it also absorbs foods through its skin. Metals and salts can be absorbed in this manner. So can many other materials, such as vitamins, fatty acids and dissolved amino acids. Metals and minerals may be concentrated and incorporated into the organic matrix or the skeleton. It is rather interesting that organic substances, especially the fatty acids, may be important foods for "dirty" water corals. (Mangrove swamps export fatty acids to reef flats and lagoons.)

In any case, drinking is a major factor in absorbing various substances for incorporation into skeletal or organic components.

Predatory Feeding

As a child, I was horrified to hear stories about "Fire corals" (Millepora). Friends told of their diving adventures and their experiences of being stung by this coral. I didn't understand how the coral stung them, I just knew that they did. Today, I know how they do it. It is with their cnidoblasts or nematocysts; it still frightens me a little. These tiny stinging cells are an identifying feature of the whole Phylum. When a particle strikes the hair-like "triggers" of a nematocyst, it "pops" open and the water rushing in displaces a tiny, thread-like needle filled with venom. The needle may puncture the target and "sting" it or it may entangle it. If the object is large, the threads break off. If the particle is too small, it may do nothing. But if the punctured particle is small and bleeds the right stuff, the coral senses this and wants to eat. The coral wants dinner when it smells amino acids or proteins. Different amino acids cause different responses among corals. What triggers a feeding response in Goniopora may not do the same for Catalaphyllia. Remember we said that nitrogen is the limiting substance for coral growth? Well, here's a great source, zooplankton, which are relatively large and about 16% nitrogen by dry weight.

What to Feed Corals

We should understand that the question is not "Do I feed my corals," but instead, "What do I feed my corals." Unfortunately, there is not a pat answer. In all honesty, there appear to be some corals that really don't need feeding; their foods occur naturally and in sufficient quantities within the aquarium to satisfy their needs. Others will slowly die of starvation without the aid of the aquarist. Adding food to the tank will encourage algae to grow but that is not the issue. The long term maintenance of these delicate and beautiful sea animals is what we desire. Scientists have conducted tests called respiratory quotients on many corals. The results of these tests tell them what the coral digests and, hence, what its nutritional requirements might be. If an animal is starved, it will usually exhaust its carbohydrate reserves first. Zooxanthellae produce carbohydrates, but, in all likelihood, the carbohydrate and lipid levels drop in poor lighting which is the case in quite a few reef tanks.

The carbohydrate demand of the animal is not being supplied by the zooxanthellae in poor light and the coral uses up its stored supply. Stored fats are then exhausted as the respiratory quotient drops. The coral will begin to shrink in size. When fats are gone, the animal will cannibalize itself and consume its proteins found in its tissues and organic matrix. This condition is known as kwashiorkor and is a condition also seen in starving humans. Have you ever seen starving people who were skin and bones but had bulging stomachs? These unfortunate souls have digested most of their muscle tissue including the abdominal tissues that support their internal organs. They are near death. When a coral begins to shrink, it is a good indication that lighting and/or nutrition are not sufficient. As the coral consumes its proteins, holes begin to appear and the skeleton is made bear. Algae will gain a hold and the coral's days are numbered. The coral may have survived a year in captivity. Look at it this way, would you place a fish in a bare aquarium and never feed it? Of course not. Back to the subject at hand... what to feed. You've got several choices. The first is:

Brine Shrimp

Brine shrimp are great. Their eggs are conveniently stored and hatched. Fish love 'em, corals should too, right? Yes, corals will eat brine shrimp, but they shouldn't be an only food. Newly hatched brine shrimp, called nauplii (nah-plee) may be too large for many small-polyped corals such as Acropora or Porites.

Rotifers

Rotifers are tiny aquatic invertebrate animals that are commonly cultured for raising fish larvae. They're much smaller than brine shrimp and are a good, but incomplete, food as any single source usually is. Culturing rotifers takes something of a wet "green" thumb and sometimes involves separate marine algae cultures acting as a food supply. This culture method makes rotifers very attractive as it mimics the zooplankton-eating-the-phytoplankton part of the food web we would expect to occur in the oceans. Researchers have devised a way to "turbocharge" these little guys and get their nutritional value way up. This method applies to brine shrimp too.

Enriching Live Foods

Commercial fish farms use this technique to enrich the nutritional value of various live foods and there's no reason the hobbyist can't also. About twelve hours before feeding, the rotifers or brine shrimp are placed in a gently aerated container. They are fed and allowed to incorporate the feed into their own tissues. Just what are these foods? Oils mostly, such as corn and pollock (cod) liver oils, which are very good sources of fatty acids and some fat soluble vitamins; D, for instance. But oil and water don't mix! Fish farmers use lecithin (available in drug and health food stores) to emulsify the oil and to get it to mix with water. A fairly complete vitamin/oil mixture would consist of a few drops of olive oil, corn oil, sunflower oil, cod liver oil and the fat vitamins A and E. Add a pinch of lecithin to the oils and mix thoroughtly. Add one or two milliliters to every five gallons of water containing the brine shrimp or the rotifers. Feed the animals to your corals or fish larvae in about twelve hours.

Making Your Own Coral Food

I add this section as a reference for those wishing to experiment with coral foods. This food is not inexpensive to make and results cannot be guaranteed. But I have used this type of food, or one of its variations, for about two years and believe that the lives of my captive corals have been extended. This is what you'll need. At the grocery, get several large brown shrimp and oysters. Pick up a small bottle of kelp lecithin, multivitamin supplements and, if its

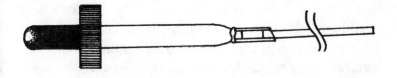

not already in the kitchen, small bottles of olive oil, corn oil, soy oil and canola oil. Also get a bottle of the most complete amino acid capsules that you can find (these usually contain about 20 amino acids). Back home, liquefy the shrimp and oysters in a blender. Add 1 tablespoon of each oil to a separate container and emulsify with a lecithin tablet. Add 1 vitamin tablet, the contents of an amino acid capsule and the emulsified oils to the blender and liquefy for a couple of minutes. If a little extra liquid is needed to get the proper depth in the blender, I add a commercially available fatty acid/vitamin supplement made for reef tanks. This concoction is poured into a small cube tray and frozen. The corals are fed once or twice a week. Large chunks go to the fleshy corals such as Euphyllia and the tiny liquidized bits go to Acropora and other small polyped corals.

How To Feed

Use a modified eye dropper to feed the corals. These are available at pet shops or you can make your own. Get an eye dropper at the pharmacy and rustle up some of that 5/16 inch rigid tubing that goes on a subsand filter. Slip the tubing over the end of the eye dropper and silicone in place. A flexible piece of tubing half way down the rigid tubing allows the tip to be pointed as desired.

When To Feed

Although this isn't really critical, try to feed in the morning after the polyps have expanded under the lights. This way, the nitrogen, phosphorus, acetate and other products of digestion are available for the zooxanthellae to use in photosynthesis during the afternoon and early evening.

The Aftermath of Feeding

Since feeding the coral aquarium is necessary, it is also a responsibility to deal with the results. Waste products will be produced in a matter of hours. These wastes will add carbon, nitrogen and phosphorus to the water. It is therefore highly recommended that the aquarist develop a realistic maintenance schedule that can be adhered to. Here's a suggested routine:

Feed the corals on Saturday or Sunday morning. While feeding, place a filter pad in the aquarium overflow to catch gross food particles. The day after feeding, siphon, or preferably, vacuum detritus. Simulate storm conditions with all water pumps running after placing the filter pad back in the overflow. Remove the pad after the storm. Do a 10% water change. Place bagged activated carbon in the overflow for two days a week.

Chapter 32

CORAL DISEASES, PREDATORS AND PARASITES

In the late 1950's, many researchers falsely believed that corals were protected by their stinging cells against natural enemies.   Increased awareness has, of course, laid that notion to rest.   We now have a modest listing of coral predators, parasites and diseases.   Careful observations by aquarists will undoubtedly expand our knowledge. Before beginning, a quick review will be made of the terminology used:

Parasitism - One organism benefits (the parasite) while another (the host) is adversely affected.   The host may exhibit reduced growth and the chance of survival may be diminished.

Predation - One organism eats another.   Of course, predation is fatal to the organism eaten if it is completely consumed.   Recovery is possible if damage is limited.

Mutualism - Both organisms benefit from the other's presence, but they are not dependent upon one another.

Commensalism - Host organism is not adversely affected while the guest organism benefits from the relationship.

Disease - Any deviation from or interruption of the normal structure or function of any body part, organ or system that is manifested by a characteristic set of symptoms.

With the definitions out of the way, our discussion will begin with common predators of corals - fishes.

Fishes Unsuitable for the Reef Aquarium

There are many reasons why a fish may not be suitable for a reef aquarium. The fish may be extremely difficult to keep. Moorish Idols are a good example. The fish may be too large and "clumsy"; any animal that might knock corals over should be excluded. In nature, the fish might have a commensal relationship with a coral. But in the aquarium the fish seeks shelter within a small coral colony and bothers it to the point that the polyps no longer expand. This commensal relation has soured; the coral may eventually die. And, of course, the fish might eat the coral or vice versa.

Coral-Eating Fishes

There are quite a few fishes that eye corals with dinner in mind. Unless the goal to keep coral-eating fishes and the inclination (and pocketbook) is there to supply the food on a consistent basis, the following fishes are best left out of the reef aquarium.

Parrotfishes

Most Parrotfishes (Scarus) are too large for the average home aquarium. Smaller specimens are seldom available. The Miami Seaquarium maintained Parrotfishes on a diet of kibbled dog food. This would be an interesting experiment for the really daring reef hobbyist. This fishes' powerful jaws scrape off a portion of the coral skeleton, along with the meaty polyps, and this is crushed and ingested. A great deal of the reef's coral sand is due to the predatory nature of these fishes.

Damselfishes

These fishes, generally described as ideal aquarium inhabitants, may not be completely safe for the reef aquarium. For example, the Three-spot Damsel (Stegastes planiforms) is known to kill corals and allow algae to grow on the skeleton. The fish eats the algae and will defend its "farm" against all would-be grazers.

Butterflyfishes

Butterflyfishes (Chaetodon) are quite common in a well stocked dealer's tank. These fishes are known to eat stony and soft corals with gusto. Species to avoid, among others, are the Ornate Butterfly (C. ornatissimus), Red Sea Melon Butterfly (C. austriacus), Baronessa Butterfly (C. baronessa), Masked Butterfly (C. larvatus), Kleins Butterfly

Several Unsuitable Butterflyfishes for the Reef Aquarium

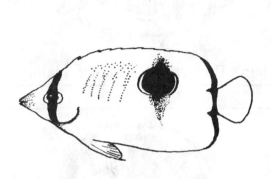

Tear Drop Butterfly (Chaetodon unimaculatus)

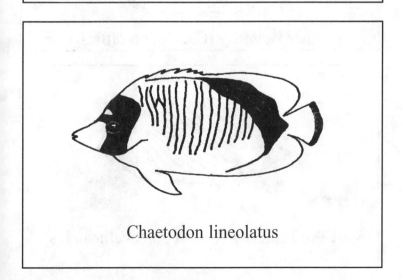

Chaetodon lineolatus

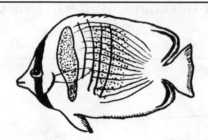

Klein's Butterfly (Chaetodon kleini)

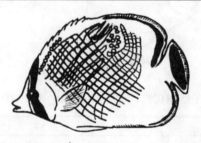

Raffle's Butterfly (Chaetodon rafflesi)

Spot Tail Butterfly (Chaetodon ocellicaudus)

(C. kleini) and the Melon Butterfly (C. trifasciatus). This listing should not be considered comprehensive.

Many other fishes will without a doubt eat corals. It should also be remembered that large solitary corals will eat fishes. Some gobies, blennies and other bottom dwelling fishes may be at risk.

Nudibranchs

These interesting animals, "snails without shells," are gastropod molluscs and are noted for their difficult nature in

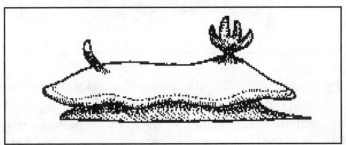

captivity. If provided with a proper diet, these animals would likely prosper in an aquarium. The familiar Sun Coral

(Tubastrea) is a special treat for the nudibranch, Phestilla. This slow moving mollusc obtains it's orange coloration from it's prey. Therefore, it is obvious and easily removed.

Other Gastropods (Snails)

Carnivorous snails pose a real threat to the coral reef aquarium. They are difficult to spot on live rock (suggesting that a curing/quarantine period is appropriate), may be imported as eggs or adults (particularly on stony corals) or may be present within the soft or stony coral when purchased. There are probably thousands of predatory gastropod molluscs; this modest listing will present a idea of the strategies these animals take.

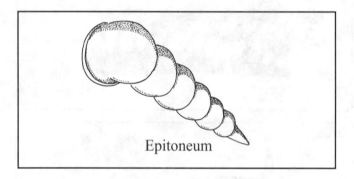

Epitoneum

Epitoneum (a wentletrap) eats the Plate coral (Heliofungia actiniformis). Epitoneum ulu is a predator of the stony Mushroom coral (Fungia scutaria). Carefully inspect the stony undersides of these corals for eggs or adult wentletraps. Many wentletraps are not harmful but removing all of them is prudent.

Another gastropod, Leptoconchus, eats the following stony corals: Flower Pot (Goniopora), Favia, Goniastrea and Echinopora. This snail will actually bore inside the coral

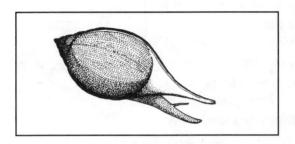

skeleton. This is not fatal in the wild but may provide a toe-hold for infections in a poorly maintained aquarium.

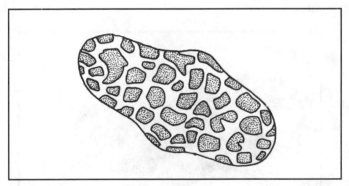

The Flamingo Tongue (Cyphoma) eats Sea Fans and Gorgonias. Although it is not noted as a stony coral pred-ator, it should not be included in the reef aquarium as it will slowly starve.

Another gastropod, Magilopsis, eats the stony corals Montipora and Cyphastrea.

The Turnip snail (Rappa rappa) is a well known predator of soft corals, particularly the Leather corals (Sarcophyton spp.) These gastropods bore into the living coral tissue and stress the coral. Reports of aquarists cutting open the coral and successfully removing the snail have

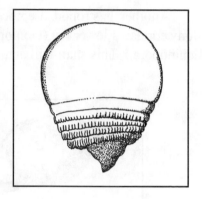

been reported. Unless the damage is severe, the Leather coral will usually recover. It may be that the Turnip snail actually spreads soft corals via the reproductive strategy known as fragmentation.

Some cowries are predators of the shallow water soft coral, Sinularia. The White Egg cowrie is known to eat Leather corals (Sarcophyton).

Flatworms

Flatworms are primitive animals and certain free-living forms (Turbellarians) are coral commensals and parasites. The commensals are known to infest the Elegance (Catalaphyllia) and Plate (Heliofungia) corals as well as Montipora, Lobophyllia, Stylophora and Hydroplana. These flatworms probably eat the coral's energy-rich mucus coating and do not harm it. One of the known parasitic flatworms is Prosthiostomum, which has an affinity for several Montipora species. This flatworm grows to a maximum length of 18 mm (about 3/4 inch) under favorable conditions.  This animal may be difficult to spot since it assumes the color of its host. In addition, this flatworm doesnot favor bright light and eats only the shaded portion of the coral. Infestations are linked to pollution caused by municipal sewage discharges, which presumably cause a rise in phosphorus and nitrate levels, 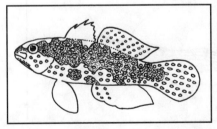 as well as depressing the dissolved oxygen content. Optimal temperature is 27°C (80.6°F). Under these conditions, the flatworms may literally cover the coral, thereby preventing it from getting sufficient light and blocking effective polyp expansion. Flatworm infestations can be controlled, but not eliminated, by lowering. the water temperature to about 23.6°C (about 74°F).

Prosthiostomum reportedly is eaten by Parrotfishes (which are also excellent at coral control!), the Tang, Acanthurus saudvicensis, and the Starryfin Goby (Asteropteryx semipunctatus).   Dipping the coral in freshwater for a minute or two will also offer relief for flat-worm infestations.

Crabs and Shrimp

Very few crabs can be recommend-ed for the reef aquarium.   Large hermit crabs, blue crabs and stone crabs are to be avoided.   Small al-gae-eating crabs such as the Three-color hermit crab (Clibanarius tri-color) (left) can be recommended as can the Urchin crab (Percnon gibbesi) - see drawing in Chapter 6.

Some shrimps are usually okay for the coral reef tank al-though they have a bad habit of snatching food away from corals at-tempting to feed.   The Peppermint shrimp (Lysmata) is a predator of the Leather corals (Sarcophyton).

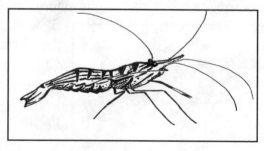

Mantis shrimp (Gonodactylus and Squilla) should also be avoided.

Some shrimps and crabs are natural predators of the Bristleworm and will be discussed below.

Fire or Bristle Worms

Hermodice, the Fire or Bristle worm is a known predator of corals. Like many pests, they are often imported into the tank on live rock. These segemented worms, which can

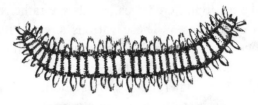

grow to about one foot in length, present a menace to stony corals, anemones as well as the hobbyist. A most unpleasant burning sensation will be experienced by anyone unfortunate enough to make contact with the short bristles extending from both sides of the animal. Controlling Fire worms can be accomplished naturally by adding Dottybacks (Pseudochromis), Arrow crabs (Stenorhynchus seticornis) or Banded Coral Shrimps (Stenopus hispidus). Fire worm traps especially designed for aquarium use are commercially available.

Coral Diseases

Coral diseases have only recently been investigated. Some maladies are stress related, others are an infestation of some sort. In other cases, the causes are unknown and only the symptoms have been described.

Bacterial Infections

Like all living creatures, corals are rather adaptive to stressful conditions. These various stresses may include emergence (exposure to the atmosphere), high or low temperature, excessive nutrient levels, irritation by various chemicals or a synergistic combination. Many corals respond to these stresses by secreting mucus. This very effective mechanism has been known to protect corals for days from copper sulfate in concentrations of up to 1,000 parts per million. If the stress continues, the coral will be weakened and, ironically, the protective mucus envelope will prove to be its undoing. The mucus is an excellent high energy food stuff and, as the coral secretes more, natural bacterial populations explode proportionally. The bacteria compete with the coral for oxygen and the coral will eventually lose. Obviously, preventing stressful situations is the key.

Black Band Disease

The root cause of this disease is stress. Black Band disease is actually an infestation of the blue-green algae Oscillatoria submembranacea and Phormidium corallyticum.

Stony corals subject to the disease include Favia, Diploria, Montastrea, Siderastrea and Porites. Octocorals affected are Gorgonia ventalina and G. flabellum. The infection begins when the algae filaments insert themselves into the coral's mouth. They multiply and eventually form a dark band that marches across the coral, killing tissue as it goes. The dead coral serves as a food source not only for the algae, but for predatory bacteria, copepods and nematodes, as well. The "black band" is in stark contrast to the white coral skeleton left behind. Small corals will be killed in a matter of days. Larger coral heads are likely to escape total destruction as the infection will usually stop as it approaches the vertical portions of the coral.

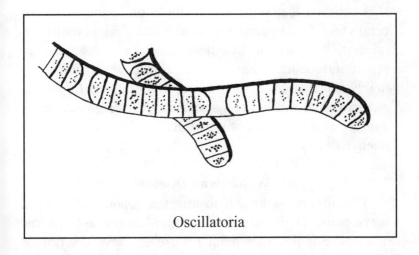

Oscillatoria

Black Band Disease Treatment

Fortunately, drugs to combat this ailment are available at pet shops. Penicillin, erythromycin and streptomycin have all been found to be effective. Antibiotics in general (and erythromycin in particular) tend to inhibit the critical carbonaceous and nitrogenous bacteria in the show aquarium; therefore, treatment should take place in a hospital tank. The successful dosage will depend upon the degree of infestation. Begin with the product's recommended dosage and, if no improvement is noted in 24 hours, dose again with slightly more medication and so on.

Shut Down Syndrome

Besides the symptoms, little is known about this ailment. It is believed that some sort of infection begins when the coral's tissue is damaged, say, by a scratch. Rapid tissue disintegration occurs and, in extreme cases, can actually be observed advancing. Even worse, Shut down Syndrome is highly contagious. Goniopora, Heliofungia, Euphyllia, Acropora and others are suspectable. If diagnosed early, antibiotics may prove successful for the experimenting hobbyist.

White Band Disease

This disease is known to affect Acropora palmata, A. cervicornis, Diploria strigosa and Montastrea annularis. The cause is not known,but researchers have determined elevated nutrient levels (nitrates and phosphates) do not seem to seem to play a role. Therefore, it seems likely an algae infestation can be ruled out. Loss of tissue occurs slowly: 1mm to 3mm (1/25 to 1/8 inch) per day is average. As the disease advances, the coral's white skeleton is exposed. No discolored band (as in Black Band disease) has been noted. The cure, like the cause, is unknown.

Corals are reported to suffer from a form of cancer. If this is the case, it would appear corals are subject to a variety of afflications ranging from preventable to treatable to fatal. We still have a lot to learn.

Chapter 33

AGGRESSION

Travel brochures describe the tropical paradise as a tranquil haven, a spot to escape the pressures of life. The vacationer relaxes and lazily snorkels above the calm reef, admiring its quiet beauty. It is an illusion. The coral reef is a battlefield full of toxic agents where the stakes are of life and death. It is a rat race taken to an ultimate limit - it is kill or be killed. The weapons vary. Foot-long stinging harpoons, filaments spreading organic acids and various deadly chemicals. Sometimes the battle is won by the quick; more often the victor is the one with the most lethal weapon. Every square meter of reef bottom is prized territory; it is coveted by many. When a coral planula settles upon a suitable surface, it has found a spot it can potentially occupy for decades if not centuries. This initial step is only the opening round. Its fight has just begun.

A coral's life in the aquarium is not much different.

Chemical Warfare

All corals have a chemical signature. These chemicals are called terpenes (which are a form of fat). Certainly an odd sounding name for substances that are very familiar to us. Common terpenes are lemonene (lemon oil) and turpentine (from pine trees). The fat soluble vitamins A, E and K are turpenes.

Many turpenes have been isolated from various corals, but the majority of research has been done on soft corals. For instance, the Leather coral (Sarcophyton) contains sarcophene. This substance is part of the mucus skin these animals shed and can be toxic to fishes at a concentration of as little as 3 parts per million. Fishes affected by sarcophene poisoning exhibit these symptoms: excitation, jumping, floating, sinking and ultimately, death. (Fishes moved to unpolluted water at the first sign of these symptoms will normally recover). All soft corals release terpenes with common ones being Lobolide (from Lobophytum) and Africanol (from Lemnalia). Some terpenes repel coral-eating fishes. Others inhibit the growth of micro-algae and potential parasites. Not all terpenes are toxic. The terpenes contained in various Staghorn corals (Acropora) give them distinctive odors; so distinctive, in fact, that real coral experts identify Acropora species by smell! Other corals "identify" the scent of other corals and react in different ways. Some will not react at all; they are not sensitive to a specific terpene. Those that are sensitive may only react minimally by failing to expand fully. Others may exhibit allergy-like symptoms, such as extra mucus production. Stronger reactions (usually between different species) may result in a chronic troubling of a submissive animal. In extreme cases, the tissue of a coral may actually be dissolved by terpenes.

Other corals deliver warnings to trespassers via stings not unlike those of wasps. To adequately "patrol" their territories, many stony corals will extend specialized processes called sweeper tentacles.   Often stretching half a foot in length, they extend in the currents and will sting any animal unfortunate enough to come within striking distance. The sweepers of some corals (such as the Bubble coral - Plerogyra) may simply brush the offender. Others, such as the Anchor coral (Euphyllia) vigorously attack, imbed and then break off in the victim specialized stinging tips.   The Euphyllia will generally regenerate a new stinging tip within a few weeks time. (See aggression listing.)

Overgrowth

A survival strategy of many soft corals, zoanthids and a few stony corals is one of overgrowth.   This method is simple and effective.   Zoanthids such as the Colonial "Anemone" (Palythoa) and the Green Sea Mat (Zoanthus) grow quickly and cover stony corals, smothering them as they go (a process called "overtopping").   Lateral aggression is also a form of overgrowth. Some stony corals do this by using toxins to dissolve the tissues of the subordinate coral. Zoanthids do also (Palythoa uses a toxin called Palytoxin).

Another overgrowth strategy is one in which the animals competing for space never touch. Some table shaped corals use this method most effectively. The area where these corals attach to the substrate is quite small, but as the animal grows it covers its competitors, thereby denying them sufficient light or water movement. These overgrowth techniques are illustrated later in this chapter.

Mesenterial Filaments

Mesenterial filaments are internal "gut" filaments usually associated with digestion. Under certain circumstances, corals may extrude these organs through the mouth or temporary openings in the body wall. This might occur for feeding purposes or for defense. In the latter case, these filament may discharge digestive acids to dissolve any foe. Corals utilizing this strategy include the Star coral (Favia), the Open Brain coral (Trachyphyllia), Hydnophora, Acanthastrea, Platygyra and many others.

Prevention

Properly placing corals in the aquarium can be the difference between a thriving coral and a dead one. Generally, corals of the same species can be placed together and occasional touching will do no harm. It is possible to estimate the spacing required between corals by knowing the aggressiveness of the animal.

In the case of "fleshy" corals (such as Catalaphyllia and Euphyllia), allow half the width of the widest part of the skeleton between neighbors. The Flower Pot coral, (Goniopora), should be 5 times its skeletal diameter away from its closest tank mate.

In the case of stony corals without a lot of tissue (i.e., the Staghorn coral, Acropora), the reach of sweeper tentacles/mesenterial filaments can be loosely estimated by measuring the callice (the coral polyp "cup"). A one or two inch seperation is usually sufficient. In general, the smaller the callice, the smaller the sweeper tentacle.

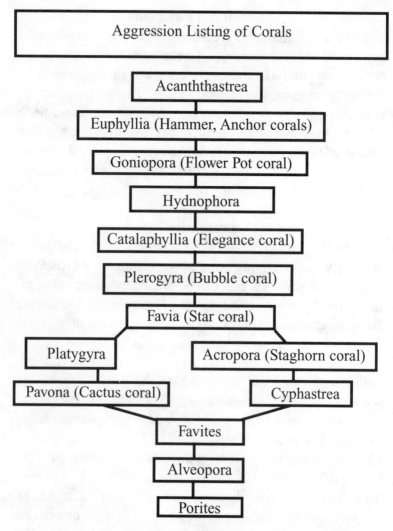

Aggression Listing of Corals

Acanththastrea

Euphyllia (Hammer, Anchor corals)

Goniopora (Flower Pot coral)

Hydnophora

Catalaphyllia (Elegance coral)

Plerogyra (Bubble coral)

Favia (Star coral)

Platygyra

Acropora (Staghorn coral)

Pavona (Cactus coral)

Cyphastrea

Favites

Alveopora

Porites

General guidelines to aggressiveness of corals. Corals in the circle interact with no particular dominance over another coral in the circle.

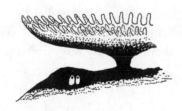

Types of Overgrowth
Top: Overtopping
Center: Lateral Aggression
Bottom: Shading

Chapter 34

REPRODUCTION

In the future, we may look back and thank some of the misinformed environmental groups for forcing limitations on the amount of live rock and number of corals collected and offered for sale in the pet industry.   Due to this pressure from the environmentalists, we are beginning to see small commercial coral breeding programs and, remarkably, good success with the propagating of both soft and stony corals at the serious hobbyist level.   These successes for the hobbyist will be claimed as a victory for the environmental groups as well, while the much greater problems of siltation due to dredging or land run-off, pollution, oil spills, destructive anchorage, etc. remain unresolved.   Perhaps the well meaning but misguided groups will realize that they had turned upon themselves by targeting aquarists who have the same goal.   And that goal is the preservation of the reefs.

Coral Reproduction

We humans sometimes suffer from the "like us" syndrome; that is, we lend "human" traits to animals.   Humans reproduce sexually, therefore, that is the norm, the standard that all animals must use.   Anything different is bizarre. From this view point, corals have to be one of the most outlandish collection of creatures on earth.

Sexual Reproduction

Boy coral meets girl coral, find that they are compatible and begin a life of devotion, making little corals along the way. Well, not exactly; really more like: Uncontrollable, raging hormones trigger a night of wild orgies. The only restraint is reproduction must occur with one of the same species. A little on the wild side, but a form of reproduction easily understood. With corals, sexual reproduction usually falls into one of two categories: brooding and broadcast spawning. Brooding has the coral egg fertilized within the polyp and there it stays until larva, or planula, are released. Some soft coral eggs are fertilized externally but the eggs brood on the coral's surface. Broadcast spawning occurs when eggs and sperm are ejected into the water column and fertilization takes place there. Broadcast spawnings are the dominate form of reproduction in the Pacific and Red Sea, while brooding predominates in the Caribbean. Many soft and stony corals use this strategy and their young develop planktonically. Broadcast spawning is a little different but not at all a difficult thing to comprehend. However, things get stranger. Much stranger. Some corals function as male and females at the same time; a condition known as hermaphroditism. Sexual organs (the ovaries and spermaries) may form on the same mesentery (See Figure 3) and occurs in favid corals such as Goniastrea and Favia. Separate sex organs may occur within the same polyp but on different mesenteries. Acropora is an example. A coral colony may possess separate male and female polyps.

Some corals are initially females, and as they mature, develop male polyps or mesenteries and become functioning hermaphrodites. Some colonies only develop a second sex during the spawning season. Self fertilization is known to occur in some Goniastrea and Acropora species. In others, the egg may act only as a buoyant carrier of sperm packets. Scientists have estimated that 70% of the world's corals are hermaphroditic.

Asexual Reproduction

Asexual reproduction occurs when there is no union between individuals or gametes. To complicate things, corals that use asexual reproduction may procreate sexually, as well.

Our discussion of asexual reproduction begins with:

Polyp Bail-Out

I didn't make this name up; it really is an accepted term among coral researchers. This reproductive strategy has only recently been described and there is little data available. Naturally, there is disagreement as to its cause. Some think it is a stress induced phenomena; others don't. All agree that it is a form of reproduction. The method is quite simple. A part of the fleshy portion of the polyp detaches from the skeleton and settles elsewhere as a new colony. Apparently, no portion of the skeleton is carried and must be reformed. This method has been observed in nature with the Bush coral (Seriatopora hystrix) and recently with an Elegance coral (Catalaphyllia) in an aquarium.

Fragmentation

Another form of asexual reproduction is fragmentation and is straightforward; a piece of the parent colony breaks off and forms a new colony. Fragmentation is a known reproductive strategy for both stony and soft corals. It differs from polyp bail-out in that a portion of the skeleton (in stony corals) is carried along. Fragmentation is known to occur with Acropora and Pavona, it likely occurs with other stony corals as well. Acropora's dominance on some reefs is attributed to fragmentation: when heavy seas break an Acropora colony to pieces, the colony may not be killed, but, in fact, spreads to new colonization points. Bioerosion may also cause fragmentation, i.e., the boring activities and subsequent weakening of the coral skeleton by the endolithic algae Ostreobium and/or the boring sponge Cliona (among others) may cause the coral to break apart.

In soft corals, fragmentation is a common reproductive strategy. Often, strong water currents are enough to break fragile soft corals to pieces, which are then dispersed by the flow. Fragmentation can occur by other means. For example, shallow-water soft and stony corals may be battered by driftwood (especially during the monsoon season) and are literally crushed to tiny fragments. Many pieces will become new colonies.

Budding

Budding is the reproductive strategy in which a new colony (called a satellite or daughter colony) forms on the body of the parent coral. Later, the satellite colony drops off to become an independent colony.

It is probable that the length of the maturation process before drop-off depends upon how fast a calcium nucleus is formed in the new coral. Technically, there are two types of budding: intratenacular and extratenacular. The difference is merely where the satellite colony forms on the parent's skeleton. Goniopora, Fungia and Favia are known to use this method of reproduction. Sarcophyton soft corals often bud as do the pesky Rock anemone (Aiptasia).

Tips on Coral Reproduction in the Aquarium

Should a coral reproduce within your aquarium, be sure to document the occurrence with color photographs, drawings and copious notes. This information should be shared with other aquarists. At a minimum, this data should include the date and time, temperature, light intensities and type of light (natural or artificial), moon phase, method of water circulation employed, feeding and chemical and other physical parameters.

If it is your goal to breed corals, be sure to exclude those fishes known to eat coral eggs or planulae. This category includes, among others, damsel fishes.

Provide the best conditions possible for your captive corals and be diligent; when the corals are happy, they will reproduce. A partial list of stony corals that have spawned in aquaria includes: Acropora, Catalaphyllia, Euphyllia, Fungia, Goniopora, Pocillopora, Trachyphyllia and Tubastrea.

Notes on Raising Coral Fragments

Acropora will be our example for fragmentation as it is especially common for the arborescent or tree-like forms of Staghorn corals to colonize reefs in this manner.

The chance of success is improved if the fragment is relatively large. Best results will be had if the broken end of the fragment is placed in a natural (or deliberately drilled) hole in a calcium based substrate, such as live rock. By placing the fragment in a hole, we have done two things: first, the coral is stabilized and second, the end is shaded and the chance of undesirable algae growth on the exposed skeleton is reduced. If conditions are correct, the fragment should have attached itself to the substrate within a week or two. Underwater epoxies and cements (including SuperGlue) are also reported to work well in securing corals to various substrates. Sometimes, the growing coral tissue will completely bridge the hole and rapidly calcify and fill it with new skeleton.

Of course, conditions will vary from species to species, but I have had best luck when the fragments receive light of about 16,000 lux and good water flow. The fragments will rapidly change their shape to maximize the amount of light falling upon them. Living tissue that is shaded from the light will slowly die off as the shape changes.

Unfortunately, some Acropora fragments suffer and die from a malady in which all tissues disintegrate. Unless the colonies are touching, this illness does not seem to be contagious.

Propagating Soft Corals

The hobbyist can easily propagate many soft corals. The materials needed are readily available - scissors or shears, single-edged safety razor blades, rubber bands, fishing line and sewing needles.

Encrusting forms of soft corals, such as the Star Polyps (Clavularia), can be simply cut into pieces. Using a razor blade, cut a small circle or square of tissue from the center of a parent colony and gently peel the "new" colony away. Secure this colony to a clean piece of live rock with a rubber band or fishing line. Attachment will occur within days if conditions are proper.

Tree-like soft corals, such as Dead Man's Hand (Sinularia), can be "pruned" of branches. Use a razor blade on large branches and sharp scissors or shears on smaller branches. Discard the razor blade after each use; carefully clean the scissors after use and keep them sharpened.

Attach the daughter colonies to live rock, empty mollusc shells and other substrates with fishing line or rubber bands.

The Leather corals (Sarcophyton) require a slightly different technique. With a razor blade, cut away part of the tentacled disk away. Attach the cutting to a small piece of live rock with a needle and nylon fishing line.

Polyp Bail-Out and Budding
Since the only significant difference seems to be the presence of a skeleton, these can generally be addressed in the same manner. The most important thing is to provide the "babies" with a protected environment. Failure to do so could result in the new colonies being swept by currents into caves or crevices of the live rock, never to be seen again.

Other than that, treat the small colony exactly as the adult.

Sexual Reproduction
It is possible that sexual reproduction by corals has occurred in many reef tanks and simply has not been observed. Corals, like all living things, have a instinct to preserve the species, and have developed strategies to strengthen the chance of successful spawnings. Corals usually spawn at night to lessen the possibility of the eggs being eaten by predators. They also do so at low tide, when there is simply less water available to dilute the gametes. Many researchers believe that the moon phase is the key to triggering a night spawning. (Incidentally, it is believed that reef flat corals, those exposed to the harshest environment where survival is a tide-to-tide fight, spawn daily in order to perpetuate their kind.

Those from deeper waters seem to have developed a monthly or annual spawning pattern.) It is known that the varying, cyclic light "resets" biological clocks in some plants and this may be the case with some corals, as well. Exactly how the coral senses the light is not known. Some scientists have speculated corals possess photorecepters (primitive "eyes"); however, the presence of these organs has not been confirmed.

An Artificial Moon for the Reef Tank

A quite simple and inexpensive artificial moon can be constructed by the handy aquarist.

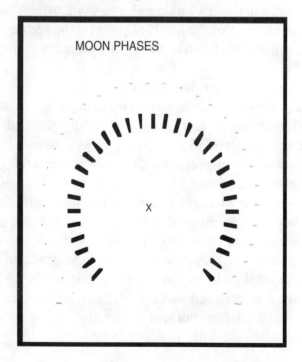

A small, incandescent "blue" bulb (the type sold as "mood" lights for fresh water aquaria or those sold as "party" bulbs in hardware stores) can be dimmed manually to simulate the moon phase and its associated light intensity.   A timer can be adjusted to turn the bulb on and off to simulate the moon rising and setting.   To track the moon phase, simply copy and secure the "moon phase" drawing on the dimmer switch cover.   Be sure to adjust the dimmer daily.

Feeding Coral Planulae

Not much data is available on rearing coral planulae. Some researchers, however, suggest that the best strategy is to remove the planulae and place them in a small tank.   Provide good lighting for the zooxanthallae, feed at least daily (brine shrimp nauplii was mentioned in one paper; enriched rotifers would probably serve very small polyps well.   See the chapter on feeding for details on enriching food stuffs).   The rearing container would be cleaned daily and any excess food or dead planulae should be removed.   It should be noted that unfed planulae die, which, of course, suggests that feeding is necessary.

Spawning Habits of Various Corals

Actinodiscus

Reproduce asexually via budding with reports that fragmentation is a reproductive strategy as well.   Also reproduce sexually.

Acropora

Some species spawn year round with no noted periodicity. Almost without exception, they are hermaphroditic spawners. Only rarely are hermaphroditic brooders. Slow extrusion of white, red, pink, cream or orange eggs occurs in darkness. Uses the fragmentation process, also.

Catalaphyllia

Individual specimens are either male or female. Are broad cast spawners when reproducing sexually. Reproduces asexually via Polyp Bail-Out.

Clavularia

Reproduce sexually, but the means most observed in aquaria will be fragmentation.

Euphyllia

E. ancora and E. divisa have separate male and female colonies. Are noted to vigorously eject gametes during darkness 4 or 5 days after a full moon. Euphyllia glabrescens is known to brood planula; it is not known if these are produced hermaphroditically.

Favia

Favia fragum is noted to brood planula and extrude them year round. In other locations, they release eggs and sperm. Favia pallida's gonads ripen with rising water temperature and is usually an hermaphroditic spawner. It is generally believed that Favia species do not mature sexually until about 8 years of age.

Fungia

Reproduces sexually or asexually by producing daughter colonies called acanthocauli.

Goniastrea

Hermaphroditic brooder or spawner according to locale. Goniastrea aspera reproduces during the spring on full and new moon phases. It expels buoyant egg packets while G. fabulous extrudes sticky eggs and sperm separately.

Goniopora

Reproduces sexually or asexually. Vigorously ejects gametes (eggs are brown or tan) four to eight days after a full moon. Asexually produces daughter colonies via extratenacular budding.

Heliofungia

One reference notes Heliofungia to spawn as separate male and female colonies; another observed planulation with a new moon during winter, spring and fall. Only colonies greater than 8 cm. (about 3.2 inches) in diameter reproduce. These colonies are estimated to be 10 years old.

Hydnophora

Hermaphroditic spawner in darkness with passive release of gametes.

Lobophytum

Known to reproduce sexually. Sexually maturity is noted when colonies are 18 cm (7 inches) across. Likely to reproduce via fragmentation.

Pavona

Reproduce sexually and asexually (via budding and fragmentation). Male and female colonies are seperate. Spawn during the spring.

Sarcophyton
A sexual reproduction including budding and fragmentation. Also reproduces sexually.

Sinularia
Sexual and asexual means are utilized.

Trachyphyllia
Broad cast spawner.

Tubipora
Little information is available concerning this animal's reproductive habits. It undoubtedly reproduces sexually. Since many colonies offered for sale have been broken from larger colonies, it is likely that fragmentation is a successful strategy, as well.

Tubastrea
Noted to have seperate female and male colonies by one researcher. Also noted to release orange planula (2 mm long) in the late summer through late fall.

Turbinaria
Reported as sexual spawners only. Thought to reproduce only once a year, during the fall.

Xenia
Various asexual methods are used as well as sexual reproduction.

APPENDIX

I offer the results of some rather lengthy testing of various aquaria lights. I wish to state that these figures should not be considered absolute since many variables can affect the amount of light emitted by a particular source. Even more variables can affect the amount of light actually falling upon a coral housed within the aquarium. These figures are offered only to replace the inadequate terms such "low light" and "bright light."

All bulbs were new when tested although the metal halides were burned for 100 hours before the readings were taken. No luminaire lenses were used on the fluorescent lights; the metal halide luminaire used a standard plastic "UV shield" lens. Reflective luminaire surfaces were flat white. Standard fluorescent bulbs (40 watt) had no internal reflectors. V.H.O. fluorescents did contain the 180 degree internal reflectors and were powered by an electronic ballast.

With the exception of the LiCor quantum meter, no equipment used that is not readily available to the reef tank hobbyist.

All readings are expressed in lux. If conversions are desired, use the following formulas:

> 1 lux = 1 lumen per square meter
> 1 lux = 1 metercandle
> 1 footcandle = 0.0929 lux

To convert lux readings to Photosynthetically Active Radiation (P.A.R.), use the following factors. They will provide approximate (and conservative) P.A.R. values. However, these conservative numbers are likely to allow a margin for lumen depreciation, that is, these readings are likely to be those of an older bulb instead of a brand new one.

> Metal Halide P.A.R.= Lux divided by 75
> 10,000 K Metal Halide P.A.R.= Lux divided by 30
> "Reef " Fluorescent Bulb P.A.R. = Lux divided by 54
> Actinic Fluorescent Bulb P.A.R.= Lux divided by 18

A 70-gallon aquarium was used in these tests. The bulbs were 4 inches to 4.5 inches above the water's surface. Readings were taken every 6 inches, both horizontally and vertically.

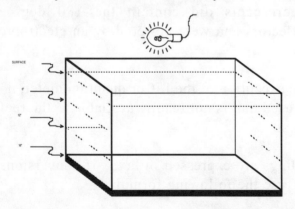

Two 175-watt Metal Halide Bulbs (6,500 K)
Approximate Lux at Various Depths

At the Water's Surface
Back

8100	12880	16840	14510	9450	17220	16380	11310	8150
10640	18820	24500	20000	16930	27200	31700	22000	14050
10060	18360	22800	18300	18400	26700	31700	20300	13300
6680	10800	14760	13420	12420	20700	19700	11610	10020

Front

6 Inches Below the Surface
Back

9275	9050	8670	7740	9705	9605	9455	8805	9905
7180	6965	6410	5680	7405	7255	7455	6935	7880
7845	7060	6695	6005	8135	8090		7925	6785	8060
8965	7645	9295	7300	8755	10280	9320	8890	9865

Front

12 Inches Below the Surface
Back

8860	8215	8935	9515	9560	8815	10205	8855	9160
7860	6860	7925	8640	8895	8520	9650	8355	8450
7880	7135	8205	8700	9170	8810	9805	8405	8650
8980	7960	9325	10380	1164	11100	12467	10815	11720

Front

18 Inches Below the Surface
Back

8620	8310	7638	7303	8670	8188	8065	9260	9380
7628	6963	6573	6948	7288	7135	7085	8393	8260
6918	6655	6925	6598	7700	6723	7368	8083	8368
6920	8210	7415	8350	8355	7545	7665	9285	8430

Front

Four 110-watt V.H.O. Fluorescent Tubes
Approximate Lux Readings at Various Depths

At the Water's Surface
Back

6240	9600	11240	11310	9830	11940	10200	8050	5060
7900	12840	14350	14790	9930	14870	12660	9560	5090
8020	12130	13940	14310	12420	14480	12610	9230	5710
5060	8720	9450	10050	6790	10280	8870	6530	4640

Front

6 Inches Below Surface
Back

9160	9450	12500	13050	10100	11790	12150	10770	7610
8400	9210	11710	11330	9580	10550	10480	8600	7050
8150	10340	11120	10630	9570	10340	9900	8170	6900
7190	8040	9980	10480	9440	10150	9820	7620	6810

Front

12 Inches Below Surface								
Back								
9560	9600	10440	10520	10100	9640	9270	7880	7050
7700	8120	9280	8980	8640	8500	8130	6730	6430
7390	8030	8640	9400	8710	8680	8260	6930	6680
7080	7740	8880	9540	9090	9130	8690	7360	6910
Front								

18 Inches Below the Surface								
Back								
7700	7700	8180	8440	8660	8160	7740	7100	6840
7600	7700	7640	8160	8220	8090	7580	7020	6950
6450	6740	8150	8160	8160	7900	7350	6990	6720
6440	6800	6920	7920	7780	7540	6940	6850	6380
Front								

Two 110-watt V.H.O. "Reef" Fluorescent Bulbs
Approximate Lux Readings

At The Water's Surface

Back

4210	7270	9170	9180	6420	9800	8570	7170	4240
4960	8140	9620	10000	7520	9060	7940	6760	3920
4510	8180	10110	9760	9300	10500	8080	6390	4130
3750	4700	6430	6190	4170	5460	5060	2700	1860

Front

6 Inches Below Surface

Back

5020	6430	7350	7500	6630	7220	7360	6260	4670
4850	5540	7030	7150	6170	6490	6860	5540	5570
4750	5610	6300	6790	5920	6450	6010	5150	4180
4330	5130	5510	6230	5390	5570	5220	4810	3900

Front

12 Inches Below the Surface								
Back								
5920	5820	6820	6900	6800	6920	6760	5880	5460
4930	5310	6240	6180	5700	5950	5650	4960	4760
5080	5420	6120	6210	5970	5890	5550	4970	4890
5190	5580	6070	6360	6010	5760	5460	4900	4720
Front								

18 Inches Below the Surface								
Back								
5410	5500	5750	5990	5890	5780	5470	5290	4990
5410	5290	5690	5770	5860	5470	5380	5230	4910
4900	4900	5150	5620	5540	5400	5070	4630	4400
4560	4920	5180	5390	5130	5050	4810	4790	4290
Front								

Four 40-watt V.H.O. "Reef" Fluorescent Bulbs (2 Actinics, 2 Daylights) Approximate Lux Readings

At The Water's Surface

			Back					
1679	3040	3590	3660	2850	3660	3460	3020	2020
3130	5380	5240	5420	5040	5760	5180	4460	2680
2910	4960	6050	6040	5250	5850	5820	4420	2810
1412	2630	2800	2710	2510	2490	1989	1570	1087

Front

6 Inches Below Surface

			Back					
2840	3410	3960	3890	3450	3860	7360	6260	4670
2620	3260	3810	3710	3280	3620	3630	3090	2710
2570	2880	3540	3600	3220	3620	3650	3000	2620
2450	2850	3440	3440	3130	3510	3410	2760	2600

Front

```
┌─────────────────────────────────────────────────────────┐
│              12 Inches Below the Surface                  │
│                        Back                               │
│  2890  3030  3350  3510  3420  3450  3510    3220   2980  │
│                                                           │
│  2410  2580  3100  3160  3120  3230  3170    2820   2620  │
│                                                           │
│  2480  2560  3000  3100  3050  3070  2860    2640   2590  │
│                                                           │
│  2470  2690  3180  3190  3050  3050  3160    2750   2530  │
│                        Front                              │
└─────────────────────────────────────────────────────────┘
```

```
┌─────────────────────────────────────────────────────────┐
│              18 Inches Below the Surface                  │
│                        Back                               │
│  2530  2570  2680  2820  2810  2830  2740    2670   2600  │
│                                                           │
│  2550  2580  2760  2920  2950  2900  2770    2690   2700  │
│                                                           │
│  2020  2110  2260  2710  2740  2740  2630    2520   2480  │
│                                                           │
│  2000  2130  2250  2690  2720  2660  2550    2440   2350  │
│                        Front                              │
└─────────────────────────────────────────────────────────┘
```

Two 40-watt Daylight Fluorescent Bulbs
Approximate Lux Readings

At the Water's Surface
Back

725	1464	1681	1646	1392	1699	1594	1362	1085
1802	3150	3330	3040	2830	2970	2600	2350	1810
2730	4030	4330	4440	4140	4380	4270	3190	2490
950	2130	2300	2370	2390	2500	2270	1660	1020

Front

Six Inches Below the Surface
Back

1810	2030	2490	2500	2220	2490	2480	2150	1930
1890	2320	2510	2410	2070	2460	2510	2060	1760
1600	1760	2320	2040	2000	2230	1970	1850	1480
1470	1720	1820	2140	1680	1800	2040	1750	1570

Front

12 Inches Below the Water's Surface
Back

1670	1820	2040	2120	2070	2090	2000	1900	1840
1580	1700	1910	1760	1910	1940	1920	1820	1760
1520	1680	1940	2010	1940	1960	1870	1740	1720
1600	1740	2060	2160	2110	2090	1880	1830	1740

Front

18 Inches Below the Water's Surface
Back

1820	1920	2020	2090	2100	2090	2020	1990	1940
1740	1810	2080	2180	2190	2190	2120	2040	2020
1560	1760	1950	2030	2020	2000	1940	1870	1830
1510	1710	1750	2050	2040	1960	1860	1820	1710

Front

Finally, some lux readings were taken of a 9-watt-actinic bulb over a 10-gallon aquarium full of water. The light was suspended 4 inches above the center of the aquarium and readings were taken at 6-inch centers. The deepest readings were taken at a 10-inch depth instead of the usual 12-inch depth.

9 watt Actinic Fluorescent Bulb
Approximate Lux Readings

At the Water's Surface		
	Back	
1200	2140	1400
2710	4640	2340
1130	1150	1200
	Front	

6 Inches Below the Water's Surface		
	Back	
1400	1250	1280
2040	2160	2070
1490	1660	1880
	Front	

10 Inches Below the Water's Surface		
	Back	
1180	1200	1200
1330	1260	1440
1080	1040	1120
	Front	

REFERENCES

A

Alino, P.M., P.W. Sammarco and J.C. Coll, 1988. Studies of the feeding preferences of Chaetodon melanotus (Pisces) for soft corals (Coelenterata, Octocoralla). Proceedings of the 6th International Coral Reef Symposium, Australia, Vol. 3, 31-36.

Anderson, J. and D. Sapulette, 1981. Deep-water Renewal in Inner Ambon Bay, Ambon, Indonesia. Proceedings of the 4th International Coral Symposium, Manila. Vol. 1.

Andrews, J.C., S. Gay and P.W. Sammarco, 1988. Influence of circulation on shelf seeding patterns at Helix Reef. Proc. 6th Int. Coral Reef Symp., Australia. Vol. 2.

Antonius, A., 1981. Coral Reef Pathology: A Review. Proceedings of the 4th International Coral Symposium, Manila. Vol. 2.

—————, 1988. Distribution and dynamics of coral diseases in the Eastern Red Sea. Proc. 6th Int. Coral Reef symp., Australia.

————————, 1988.   Black band disease behavior on Red Sea Reef corals.   Proc. 6th Int. Coral Reef Symp., vol.3, 145-150.

Atkinson, S. and M.J. Atkinson, 1992.   Detection of estra-diol-17b during a mass coral spawn.   Coral Reefs 11: 33-35.

B

Badcock, R.C., 1984.   Reproduction and Distribution of Two Species of Goniastrea (Scleractinia) from the Great Barrier Reef Providence.   Coral Reefs 2, 187-195.

Badcock, R.C., G.D. Bull, P.L. Harrison, A.J. Heyward, J.K. Oliver, C.C. Wallace and B.L. Willis, 1986.   Synchronous spawnings of 105 scleractinian corals on the Great Barrier Reef.   Marine Biology 90: 379-394.

Bak, R.P.M. and S.R. Criens, 1981.   Survival after fragmen-tation of colonies of Madracis mirabilis, Acropora palmata and Acropora cervicornis (Scleractinia) and subsequent impact of a coral disease.   Proceedings of the 4th International Coral Symposium, Manila. Vol. 2.

Bosch, H.F., 1965.   A gastropod parasite of solitary corals in Hawaii.   Pac. Sci. 19:267.

Bothwell, A., 1981.   Fragmentation, a means of asexual reproduction and dispersal in the coral genus Acropora (Scleractinia:Astrocoeniida:Acroporidae): a preliminary report.   Proceedings of the 4th International Coral Symposium, Manila. Vol. 2.

Bradbury, R. and P.C. Young, 1981.   The race and the swift revisited, or is aggression between the corals important? Proceedings of the 4th International Coral Symposium, Manila. Vol. 2.

Brakel, W.H., 1979.   Small scale spatial variation in light available to coral reef benthos: quantum irradiance measurements from a Jamaican reef.   Bull. Mar. Sci., 29(3): 406-413.

Buddemeier, R., R. Scgneider and S. Smith., 1981.   The alkaline earth chemistry of corals.   Proceedings of the 4th International Coral Symposium, Manila. Vol. 2.

C

Cairns, S.D., 1988.   Asexual reproduction in solitary scleractinia.   Proc. 6th Int. Coral reef Symp., Australia. Vol. 2, 641-646.

Cofforth, M.A., 1988. The function and fate of mucous sheets produced by coelenterates. Proc. 6th Int. Coral Reef Symp., Australia.

Cole, S., 1988. Limitations on reef coral development in the Arabian Gulf; temperature and algal competition? Proc. 6th Int. Coral Reef Symp., Australia. Vol. 3, 211 - 216.

Coll, J.C. and P.W. Sammarco, 1986. Soft corals: chemistry and ecology. Oceanus, 29:33-37.

——————— and ———————, 1988. The role of secondary metabolites in the ecology of marine invertebrates : a meeting ground for chemists and biologists. Proc. 6th Int. Coral Reef Symp., Australia. Vol., 167-173.

Cope, M., 1981. Interspecific coral interactions in Hong Kong. Proceedings of the 4th International Coral Symposium, Vol. 2, Manila.

Cowey, C.B. and E.D.S. Corner, 1963. Amino acids and some other nitrogenous compounds in Calanus finmarchus. J. Mar. Biol. Ass. U.K., 43:485-493.

Cross, T.S. and B.W. Cross, 1983. U, Sr and Mg in Holocene and Pleistocene corals, A cropora palmata and Montastrea annularis. Journal of Sedimentary Petrology, Vol. 53 (2):587-594.

Barnes, D.J., 1988.   Seasonality in community productivity and calcification at Davies Reef, Central Great Barrier Reef.   Proc. 6th Int. Coral Reef Symp., Australia.   Vol.2.

Battey, J.F. and J.W. Porter, 1988.   Photoadaptation as a whole organism responses in Montastrea annularis.   Proc. 6th Int. Coral Reef Symp., Australia. Vol. 3, 79-87.

Benayahu, Y. and Y. Loya, 1977.   Space partitioning by stony corals, soft corals and benthic algae on the coral reefs of the northern Gulf of Eliat (Red Sea).   Helgolander wiss. Meeresunters. 30: 362-382.

Berwick, N.L. and P.E. Faeth, 1988.   Simulating the impacts of sewage disposal on coral reefs. Proc. 6th Int. Coral Reef Symp., Australia. Vol. 2.

Best, M.B. and G.J. Boekschotten, 1988.   Comparative qualitative studies on coral species composition in various reef sites in the Eastern Indonesian archipelago.   Proc. 6th Int. Coral Reef Symp., Australia. Vol. 3, 197-204.

Blank, R. and R.K. Trench, 1985.   Speciation in symbiotic dinoflagellates.   Science 229:656-658.

Blanquet, R.S., J.C. Nevenzel and A.A. Benson, 1979.   Acetate incorporation into the lipids of the sea anemone Anthopleura elegantissima and its associated zooxanthellae. Mar. Biol. 54, 185-194.

Carlson, B.A., 1987. Aquarium systems for living corals. Int. Zoo. Yb. 26:1-9.

Chalker, B.E., W.C. Dunlap and P.L. Jokiel, 1986. Light and corals. Oceanus 29:22-23.

Chalker, B.E. and W.C. Dunlap, 1981. Extraction and quantification of endosymbiotic algal pigments from reef building corals. Proceedings of the 4th International Coral Symposium, Vol. 2, Manila.

Chalker, B.E., W.C. Dunlap and J.K. Oliver, 1983. Bathymetric adaptations of reef building corals at Davie's Reef, Great Barrier Reef, Australia. II. Light saturation curves for photosynthesis and respiration. Mar. Biol. Ecol. 73:37 - 56.

Charpy, L. and C.J. Charpy-Rouband, 1988. Phosphorus budget in an atoll lagoon. Proc. 6th Int. Coral Reef Symp., Australia. Vol. 2

Chou, C.M., 1988. Impact of human influence on a fringing reef at Palau Hantu, Singapore. Proc. 6th Int. Coral Reef Symp., Australia, Vol. 2

Chuang, S. I., 1981. Ecology of Singapore and Malayan coral reefs - a preliminary classification. Proceedings of the 4th International Coral Symposium, Manila.

Crossland, C.J. 1987.   In situ release of mucus and DOC-lipid from the coral Acropora.   Coral Reefs 6:35-42.

——————————, 1988.   Latitudal comparisons of coral reef structure and function.   Proc. 6th Int. Coral Reef Symp., Australia.   Vol. 1, 221-226.

Crossland, C.J., D.J. Barnes, 1977.   Gas exchange studies with the staghorn coral Acropora acuminata and its zooxanthellae.   Mar. Biol. 40:185-194.

D

Dai, Chang-Feng, 1988.   Coral communities of Southern Taiwan.   Proc. 6th Int. Coral Reef Symp., Australia.   Vol.2, 647-652.

Daumas, R. and B. Thomassin, 1977.   Protein fractions in coral and zoantharian mucus: Possible evolution in coral reef environments.   Proceedings, Third International Coral Reef Symposium.   Rosenstiel School of Marine and Atmospheric Science, University of Miami, Florida.

Davies, P.S, 1984.   The role of zooxanthellae in the nutritional requirements of Pocillopora eydouxi.   Coral Reefs 2:181-186.

Dennison, W.C. and D.J. Barnes, 1988. Effect of water motion on coral photosynthesis and calcification. J. Exp. Biol. Ecol. 115:67-77.

Dinesen, Z.D. 1983. Patterns in the distribution of soft corals across the central Great Barrier Reef. Coral Reefs(1983)1:229-236

Dunlap, W.C. and B.E. Chalker, 1986. Identification and quantification of near U.V. absorbing compounds (s-320) in a hermatypic scleractinian. Coral Reefs 5:155-159.

Dunlap, W.C. and W. Bandaranayake, 1988. U-V light absorbing agents derived from tropical marine organisms of the Great Barrier reef, Australia. Proc. 6th Int. Coral Reef Symp., Vol. 3, 89-93.

Dustan, P. 1982. Depth-dependent photoadaptation by zooxanthallae of the reef coral Monastrea annularis. Marine Biology 68:253-264.

Dykens, J. and J.M. Shick, 1982. Oxygen production in the endosymbiotic algae controls superoxide dismutase activity in their animal host. Nature 297:579-580.

E

Emerson, D.N., 1967. Some aspects of the free amino acids metabolism in developing encysted embryos of Artemia salina. Comp. Biochem. Physiol., 20:245-261.

F

Falkowski, P.G. and Z. Dubinsky, 1981. Light-shade adaptation of Stylophora pistillata, a hermatypic coral from the Gulf of Eliat. Nature 289:172-174.

Findlay, R. and D. White. Effects of M. quinquiesperforata on microbes.

Fishelson, L., 1970. Littoral fauna of the Red Sea: the population of nonscleractinian anthozoans of shallow seas of the red Sea. Mar. Biol. 6:106-116.

Fishelson, L., 1973. Ecological and biological phenonema influencing coral-species composition on the reef tables at Eliat. Marine Biol. 19:183.

Fitt, W. and P. Pardy, 1981. Effects of starvation and light and dark on the energy metabolism of symbiotic and asymbiotic sea anemones, Anthopleura elegantissima. Mar. Biol. 61:199-205.

Fogg, G., 1966. The extracellular products of algae. Oceanogr. Mar. Biol. Ann. Rev. 4:195-212.

Franzisket, L., 1974. Nitrate uptake by reef corals. Int. Rev. Gesamten. Hydrobiol. 59:1-7.

Fredericks, C., 1976. Oxygen as a limiting factor in photoaxis and in intraclonal spacing of the sea anemone Anthopleura elegantissima. Mar. Biol. 38:25-28.

Fretter, V., 1953. Experiments with radioactive strontium (Sr90) on certain mollusks and polychaetes. J. Mar. Biol. Assoc. U.K., 32:367-384.

Freudenthal, H.D., 1962. Symbiodinium Gen. Nov. and Symbiodinium microadriaticum sp. nov., a zooxanthalla: Taxonomy, life cycle and morphology. J. Protozool. 9:45-52.

G

Gil-Turnes, S. and J. Corredor, 1981. Studies of photosynthetic pigments of zooxanthellae in Caribbean hermatypic corals. Proceedings of the 4th International Coral Reef Symposium, Manila.

Gladfelter, W.B., 1982. White-band disease in Acropora palmata: implications for the structure and growth of shallow reefs. Bull. Mar. Sci. 32(2): 639-643.

Glynn, P.W., 1988. Predation on coral reefs: some key processes, concepts and research directions. Proc. 6th Int. Coral Reef Symp., Australia. Vol. 1, 51-59.

Gohar, H.A.F. and G.N. Soliman, 1963. On the biology of three coralliophilids boring in living coral. Publ. Mar. Biol. Sta. Al-Ghardaga, Red Sea. 12:99-126.

Goreau, T.F., 1963. Calcium carbonate deposition by coralline algae and corals in relation to their roles as reef builders. Ann. N.Y. Acad. Sci. 109:127.

Goreau, T.F., 1959. The physiology of skeleton formation in corals. 1. A method for measuring the rates of calcium deposition. Biol. Bull. 116:59-75.

Goreau, T.F. and N.I. Goreau, 1959. The physiology of skeleton formation in corals. II. Calcium deposition by hermatypic corals under various conditions in the reef. Biol. Bull. Mar. Bio. Lab., Woods Hole, 117:239-250.

Goreau, T.F., N. Goreau and C.M. Yonge, 1971. Reef corals: autotrophs or heterotrophs? Biol. Bull. 141:247-260.

H

Hamner, W.M. and E. Wolanski, 1988. Hydrodynamic forcing functions and biological processes on coral reefs: a status review. Proc. 6th Int. Coral Reef Symp., Australia. Vol. 1, 103-1

Hassan, H. and I. Fridovich, 1980. Enzymatic basis of detoxification. (Ed. W.B. Jakoby) 311-332. Academic, N.Y.

Haywood, M. and S. Wells, 1989. The Manual of Marine Invertebrates. Tetra Press, Morris Plains, New Jersey.

Henderson, R., 1981.   In situ and micrcosm studies of diel metabolism on reef flat communities.   Proceedings of the 4th International Coral Reef Symposium, Manila.

Heyward, A.J., 1988.   Inhibitory effects of copper and zinc sulphates on fertilization in corals.   Proc. 6th Int. Coral Reef Symp., Australia.

Hinde, R., 1988.   Symbiotic nutrition and nutrient limitation.   Proc. 6th Int. Coral Reef symp., Australia.

Hodgson, G., 1988.   Potiential gamete wastage in synchronously spawning corals due to hybrid inviability.   Proc. 6th Int. Coral Reef Symp., Australia.   Vol. 2, 707-712.

Hoeksema, B.W., B.W., 1988.   Mobility of free-living fungiid corals (scleractinia), a dispersion mechanism and survival strategy in dynamic reef habitats.   Proc. 6th Int. Coral Reef Symp., Australia.   Vol. 2, 715-720.

Hovanec, T., 1993.   All about activated carbon.   Aquarium Fish, Vol.5, No. 8:54.

Hughes, T.P., 1988.   Long-term dynamics of coral reef populations: contrasting reproductive modes.   Proc. 6th Int. Coral Reef Symp., Australia.   Vol. 2, 721-724.

Hunter, C.L., 1988. Environmental cues controlling spawning in 2 Hawiian corals, Montipora verrucosa and M. digitata. Proc. 6th Int. Coral Reef Symp., Australia. Vol. 2, 727-732.

I

I.E.S. Lighting Handbook, Illum. Eng. Soc., New York, 1984.

J

Jaubert, J., 1981. Variations in the shape and the chlorophyll concentration of the scleractinian coral Synarea convexa (Verill): Two complimentary processes to adapt to light variations. Proceedings of the 4th International Coral reef Symposium, Manila.

Jerlov, N.G., 1976. Marine Optics. Elsevier Oceanography Series, Elsevier Sci. Publ. Co., New York, 231 pp.

Johannes, R.E. and K.I. Webb, 1965. Release of dissolved amino acids by marine zooplankton. Science, 150:76-77.

Jokiel, P.L., 1985. Lunar periodicity of planula release in the reef coral Pocillopora damicornis in relation to various environmental factors. Proc. 4th Int. Coral reef Congress, Tahiti. Vol. 4, 307-312.

Jokiel, P.L., 1988. Is photoadaptation a critical process in the development , function and maintenance of reef communities? Proc. 6th Int. Coral Reef Symp., Australia. Vol. 1, 187-192.

Jokiel, P.L., R.Y. Ito and P.M. Liu, 1985. Night irradiance and synchronization of lunar release of planula larvae in the reef coral Pocillopora damicornis. Marine Biology 88:167-174.

Jokiel, J.P. and S.J. Townsley, 1974. Biology of the polyclad Prosthiostomum sp., a new coral parasite from Hawaii. Pac. Sci. 28:361.

Jokiel, P.L. and R.H. York, 1982. Solar ultraviolet photobiology of the reef coral Pocillopora damicornis and symbiotic zooxanthellae. Bull. Mar. Sci. 32(1):301-315.

K

Kaplan, E., 1988. A Field Guide to Southeastern and Caribbean Seashores. Houghton Mifflin Co., Boston, Massachusetts.

Kawaguti, S., 1944a. On the physiology of coral reefs. VII. Zooxanthallae of the corals in Gymnodinium sp., Dinoflagellata; its culture in vitro. Palao Trop. Biol. Stn. Stud., 2:675-679.

Kellogg, R.B. and J.S. Patton, 1983. Lipid droplets, medium of energy exchange in the symbiotic anemone Condylactis gigantea: a model coral polyp. Marine Biology 75: 137-144.

Kinzie, R.A., P.L. Jokiel and R. York. 1984. Effects of altered spectral compositions on coral zooxanthallae associations and on zooxanthellae in vitro. Marine Biology, 78:239-248.

Knowlton, N., J.C. Lang and B.D. Keller, 1988. Fates of Staghorn coral isolates on Hurricane-damaged reefs in Jamaica: the role of predators. Proceedings 6th Int. Coral Reef Symp., Australia.

Knudsen, J.W., 1967. Trapezia and Tetralia (Decapoda, Bracyura, Xanthidae) as obligate ectoparasites of pocilloporid and acroporid corals. Pac. Sci. 21:51-57.

Kojis, B.L., 1986. Sexual reproduction in Acropora (Isopora) species (Coelenterata:Scleractinia) I. A. cuneata and A. palifera on Heron Island Reef, Great Barrier Reef. Marine Biology 91:291-309.

L

LaBoute, P., 1988. The presence of scleractinian corals and their means of adapting to a muddy environment: the Gail Bank. Proc. 6th Int. Coral Reef Symp., Australia. Vol. 3, 107-111.

Lang, J.C., R.I. Wicklund and R.F. Dill, 1988. Depth- and habitat-related bleaching of zooxanthellae in reef organisms near Lee Stocking Island, Exuma Cays, Bahamas. Proc. 6th Int. Coral Reef Symp., Australia. Vol. 3, 269-274.

Lasker, H.R., 1988. The incidence and rate of vegetative propagation among coral reef alcyonarians. Proc. 6th Int. Coral Reef Symp., Australia. Vol. 2.

Lee, R.F., 1974. Lipids of zooplankton from Bute Inlet, British Columbia. J. Fish. Res.. Board Can., 31:1577-1582.

Lehman, J.T. and J.E. Porter, 1973. Chemical activation and feeding in the reef-building coral Monastrea cavernosa. Biol. Bull. 145:140.

Leletkin, V. and V. Zvalinsky, 1981. Photosynthesis of coral zooxanthellae from different depths. Proceedings of the 4th International Coral Reef Symposium, Vol. 1, Manila.

Lesser, M.P. and J.M. Shick, 1989. Effects of irradiance and ultraviolet radiation on photoadaptation in the zooxanthellae of Aiptasia pallida: Primary production, photoinhabition and enzymatic defenses against oxygen toxicity. Mar. Biol., 102: 243-255.

——————, W.R. Stochaj, D.W. Tapley and J.M. Shick, 1990. Bleaching in coral reef anthozoans: effects of irradiance, UV and temperature on the activities of protective enzymes against active oxygen. Coral Reefs 8:225-232.

Lewis, J.B., 1974.   The importance of light and food of the reef coral Favia fragum. J. Exp. Mar. Biol. Ecol. 15:299-304.

Lewis, J.B., 1977.   Suspension feeding in Atlantic coral reefs and the importance of suspended matter as a food source.   Proc. 3rd int. Symp. coral Reefs, pp 405-408.   Ed. by D.L. Taylor, Miami: School of Marine and Atmospheric Sciences, University of Miami.

Lewis, J.B., 1981.   Estimates of secondary production of coral reefs.   Proc. 4th int. Symp. coral Reefs, Manila.

Livingston, H.D. and G. Thompson, 1971.   Trace element concentrations in some modern corals.   Limnol. Oceanogr. 16:786-796.

Loya, Y., 1972.   Community structure and species diversity of hematypic corals at Eliat, Red Sea.   Mar. Biol. 13:100-123.

Lukas, K.J., 1974.   Two species of the chlorophyte genus Ostreobium from skeletons of the Atlantic and caribbean reef corals.   Journ. Phycol., 10 (3): 331-335.

M

MacIntyre, I.G. and J.F. Marshall, 1988.   Submarine lithification in coral reefs: some facts and misconceptions.

Proc. 6th Int. Coral Reef Symp., Australia. Vol. 1, 263-272.

Massin, C., 1988. Boring corallophilidae (Mollusca, Gastropoda): coral-host relationship. Proc. 6th Int. Coral Reef Symp., Vol. 3, 177-184.

Mayzaud, P., 1973. Respiration and nitrogen excretion of zooplankton. II. Studies of the metabolic characteristics of starved animals. Mar. Biol. 21:19-28.

Meyers, P.A., 1977. Fatty acids and hydrocarbons of caribbean corals. Proceedings of the 3rd int. coral Reef Symp.

Meyers, P.A., 1979. Polyunsaturated fatty acids in corals: indicators of nutritional sources. Mar. Biol. Lett. 1:69-75.

Mitterer, R.M., 1978. Amino acid composition and metal binding capability of the skeletal protein of coral. Bull. Mar. Sci. 28:171-180.

Mohamed, M.I.H. and Z. Badaruddin, 1988. Coral reef morphology and ecology of the Malayasian east coast islands. Proc. 6th Int. Coral reef Symp., Australia. Vol. 3, 349-353.

Muscatine,L., 1967. Glycerol excretion by symbiotic algae from corals and tridacna and its control by the host. Science, 156:516-519.

Muscatine, L. and E. Cernichiari, 1969. Assimilation of photosynthetic products of zooxanthellae by coral reef. Biol. Bull. mar. biol. Lab., 137:506.

Muscatine, L., L.R. McCloskey and R.E. Marian, 1981. Estimating the daily contribution of carbon from zooxanthellae to coral animal respiration. Limnol. Oceanogr. 26:601-611.

Moe, M., 1989. The Marine Aquarium Reference, Systems and Invertebrates. Green Turtle Publications, Plantation, Fla.

Mohan, P., 1994. Light measurements in the reef aquarium - more than meets the eye. Freshwater and Marine Aquarium magazine, 17:2, 50-56.

Morrissey, M.S., Jones and V. Harriott, 1988. Nutrient cycling in the Great Barrier Reef Aquarium. Proc. 6th Int. Coral reef Symp., Australia. Vol. 2.

N

Nakamori, T., 1988. Skeletal growth model of the dendritic hermatypic corals limited by light shelter effect. Proc. 6th Int. Coral Reef Symp., Australia. Vol. 3, 113-118.

Neeman, I., L. Fishelson and Y. Kashman, 1974. Sarcophine, a new toxin from the soft coral, Sarcophyton glaucum. Toxicon, 12:593-598.

Nishihira, M., 1981.   Interaction of Alcyonaria with hermatypic corals on an Okinawan reef flat.   Abs. 4th Int. Symp. Manila, pp 46-47.

O

Ohoe, S. and Y. Kitano, 1981.   Behavior of minor elements in the transformation of coral aragonite to calcite.Abs. 4th Int. Symp. Manila.

Oliver, J.K., R.C. Babcock, P.L. Harrison and B.L. Willis, 1988.   Geographic extent of mass coral spawning: clues to ultimate casual factors.   Proc. 6th Int. Coral Reef Symp., Australia, Vol. 2.

Oliver, J.K., B.E. Chalker and W.C. Dunlap, 1983.   Bathymetric adaptations of reef building corals at Davie's Reef, Great Barrier Reef, Australia. I. Long term growth responses of Acropora formosa (Dana 1846).   Biol. Ecol. 73:11-35.

P

Patterson, M.R., K.P. Sebens and R.R. Olson, 1991.   In situ measurements of flow effect on primary production and dark respiration in reef corals.   Limnol. Oceanogr. 36:936-948.

Patton, J.S. and J.E. Burris, 1983. Lipid synthesis and extrusion by freshly isolated zooxanthellae (symbiotic algae). Mar. Biol. 75:131-136.

Patton, J.S., J.F. Battey, M.W. Rigler, J.W. Porter, C.C. Black and J.E. Burris, 1983. A comparison of the metabolism of bicarbonate 14C and acetate 1-14C and the variability of species lipid composition in coral reefs. Mar. Biol. 75:121-130.

Pearse, V.B. and L. Muscatine, 1971. Role of symbiotic algae (zooxanthallae) in coral reef calcification. Biol. Bull. 141:350.

Peters, E., 1988. Symbiosis to pathology: Are roles of microorganisms as pathogens of coral reef organisms predictable from existing knowledge? Proc. 6th Int. Coral reef Symp., Australia. Vol. , 205-209.

Peters, E., J. Opreandy and P. Yevich, 1983. Possible causal agent of White Band Disease in caribbean Acroporid corals. Journal of Invertebrate Pathology, 41:394-396.

Pichon, M., 1981. Dynamic aspects of coral reef benthic structures and zonation. Proceedings of the 4th International Coral Reef Symposium, Vol. 1, Manila.

Pingitore, N.E., Y. Tanger and A. Kwartenc, 1989. Barium variation in Acropora palmata and Montastrea annularis. Coral Reefs 8:31-36.

Pitombo, F.B., C.C. Rato and M.J.C. Belum, 1988. Species diversity and zonation pattern of hermatypic corals at two fringing reefs of Abrolonos archipelago, Brazil. Proc. 6th Int. Coral reef Symp., Vol. 2.

R

Rajasuriya, A. and M.W.R.N. DeSilva, 1988. Stony corals of fringing reefs of the western and southwestern and southern coasts of Sri Lanka. Proc. 6th Int. Coral reef Symp., Australia. Vol. 3.

Randall, R., 1981. Morphologic diversity in the scleractinian genus Acropora. Proc. 4th int. coral Reef symp., Manila.

Raven, J.A. and F.A. Smith, 1977. "Sun" and "shade" spcies of green algae: relation of cell size and environment. Photosynthetica, 11:48-55.

Richmond, R.H., 1988. Competency and dispersal potential of planula larvae of a spawning versus brooding coral. Proc. 6th Int. Coral reef Symp., Vol. 2.

Richmond, R.H. and C.L. Hunter, 1980. Review: Reproduction and recruitment of corals, comparisons among the Caribbean, the tropical Pacific and the Red Sea. Mar. Ecol. Prog. Ser. 60:185-203.

Rinkevich, B. and Y. Loya, 1983. Short term fate of photo-synthetic products in a hermatypic coral. J. exp. mar. Biol. Ecol. 73:175-184.

_____, 1987. Variability in the pattern of sexual reproduction of the coral Stylopora pistilata at Eliat, Red Sea: a long term study. Biol. Bull. mar. biol. Lab., Woods Hole, 173:335-344.

Rinkevich, B., 1989. The contribution of photosynthetic products to coral reproduction. Marine Biology, 101:259-263.

Roberts, H.H., 1988. Proposed oceanographic controls on modern Indonesian reefs: a turn-off, turn-on mechanism in a monsoonal setting. Proc. 6th Int. coral Reef Symp., Australia. Vol. 3, 529-533.

_____, A. Lugo, B. Carter and M. Simms, 1988. A cross-reef flux and shallow subsurface hydrology in modern reef corals. Proc. 6th Int. Coral reef Symp., Vol. 2.

Robertson, R., 1970. Review of the predators and parasites of stony corals with special reference to symbiotic proso-branch gastropods. Pacific Science, 24:43.

Rogers, C.S., 1983. Sublethal and lethal effects of sediments applied to common Caribbean reef corals in the field. Marine Pollution Bulletin, Vol. 14, No. 10, pp 378-382.

Ross, M.A., 1981. A quantitative study of hermatypic coral diversity and zonation at Apo Reef, Mindoro, Philipines. Proc. 4th int. coral Reef symp., Vol.2.

S

Sarano, F. and M. Pichon, 1988. Morphology and ecology of the deep forereef slope at Osprey Reef (Coral sea). Proc. 6th Int. Coral reef Symp., Australia. Vol. 2, 607-611.

Schiller, C. and G.J. Herndl, 1989. Evidence of enhanced microbial activity in the intersital space of branched corals: possible implications for coral metabolism. Coral Reefs 7:179-184.

Schlichter, D., H.W. Fricke and W. Weber, 1986. Light harvesting by wavelength transformation in a symbiotic coral of the Red sea twilight zone. Mar. Biol., 91:403-407.

Schumacher, H. and M. PLewka, 1981. The adaptive significance of mechanical properites versus morphological adjustments in skeletons of Acropora palmata and A. cervicornis (Cnidaria scleractinia). Proceedings of the 4th International Coral Reef Symposium, Vol. 2, Manila.

Scott, B.D. and H.R. Jitts, 1977. Photosynthesis of phytoplankton and zooxanthallae on a coral reef. Mar. Biol. 41:307-315.

Sebens, K., 1977. Autotrophic and heterotrophic nutrition of coral reef zoanthids. Proceedings, Third Internation Coral Reef Symposium. Rosenstiel School of Marine and Atmospheric Science. University of Miami, Florida.

Sheppard, C.R.C., 1981. "Reach" of aggressively interacting corals and relative importance of interactions at different depths. Proceedings of the 4th International Coral reef Symposium, Vol. 2, Manila.

——————————————, 1988. Similar trends, different causes: responses of corals to stressed environments in Arabian Seas. Proc. 6th Int. Coral Reef Symp., Australia. Vol. 3.

Simkiss, K., 1964a. Phosphates as a crystal poison of calcification. Biol. Rev., 39:487-505.

Simkiss, K., 1964b. The inhibitory effects of some metabolites on the precipitation of calcium carbonate from artifical and natural seawater. J. Cons. Int. Explor. Mer. 29:6-18.

Sorokin. Y.I., 1973. On the feeding of some scleractinian corals with bacteria and dissolved organic matter. J. Amer. Soc. Limnol. Oceanogr. 18:380.

——————————, 1981. Aspects of the biomass, feeding and metabolism of common corals of the great Barrier Reef, Australia. Proceedings of the 4th International Coral Reef

Symposium, Vol. 2, Manila.

Spotte, S., 1992.   Captive Seawater Fishes: Science and Technology.   Wiley Interscience, New York, N.Y.

Srinvasagam, R.T., J.E.G. Raymont, C.F. Moodie and J.K.B. Raymont, 1971.   Biochemical studies of marine zooplankton. X. The amino acid composition of Euphausa superba, Meganyctiphanes norvegica and Neomysis integer. J. Mar. Biol. Ass., U.K., 51:917-925.

Stephens, G.C., 1962.   Uptake of organic material by aquatic invertebrates. I. Uptake of glucose by solitary coral Fungia scutaria.   Biol. Bull.   123:648.

Stephenson, W., R. Endean and I. Bennett, 1958.   An ecological review of the marine fauna of Low Isles, Queensland.   Aust. J. Mar. Freshw. Res. 9:261-318.

Stimson, J.S., 1978.   Mode and timing of reproduction in some common hermatypic corals of Hawaii and Enewetak. Marine Biology, 48:173-184.

Stimson, J.S., 1987.   Location, quantity and rate of change in quantity of lipids in tissue of Hawaiian hermatypic corals. Bull. Mar. Sci. 41:889-904.

Swart, P., 1980.   The effect of seawater chemistry on the growth of some scleractinian corals.   In: Developmental and Cellular Biology of Coelenterates.   P. Targent and R. Targent, eds.   Elsevier/North Holland Biomedical.

T

Takano, S., D. Uemera and Y. Hirata, 1978. Isolation and structure of two new amino acids, Palythinol and Palythene, from the zoanthid Palythoa tuberculosa. Tetrahedron Letters, 49:4909-4912.

Thimijan, J.C. and R.D. Heins, 1983. Photometric, radio-metric and quantum units of measure: A review of procedures of interconversion. HortScience, Vol. 18, No. 6.

Thomason, J.C. and B.E. Brown, 1986. The cnidom: an in-dex of aggressive proficiency in scleractinian corals. Coral Reefs 5:93-101.

Tidball, J., 1980.   The fine structure of the gorgonin secreting cells of the Gorgonian coral Leptogorgia virgulata (Lamarck) In: Developmental and Cellular Biology of Coelenterates.

Titlyanov, E.A., 1981.   Adaptation of reef-building corals to low light intensity.   Procedings of the 4th International Coral Symposium, Vol. 2, Manila.

Titlyanov, E.A. and Y.Y. Latypov, 1991.   Light dependence in scleractinian distribution in the sublittoral zone of south China Sea islands.   Coral Reefs 10:133-138.

Titlyanov, E.A., M.G. Shaposhnikova and V.I. Zvalinskii,

1980. Photosynthesis and adaptation of corals to irradiance. I. Contents and native state of photosynthetic pigments in symbiotic microalga. Photosynthetica 14:413-421.

Tomacik, T. and F. Sander, 1985. Effects of eutrophication on reef building corals. I. Growth rate of the reef building coral Montastrea annularis. Marine Biology 87:143-155.

Tomacik, T. and F. Sander, 1987. Effects of eutrophication on reef building corals. III. Reproduction of the coral Porites porites. Marine Biology 94:77-94.

Tursch, B., J.C. Brackman, D. Daloze and M. Kaisan, 1978. Terpenoids from coelenterates. In: Marine Natural Products, Vol. II, Ed. by P.J. Schuer, New York: Academic Press.

_____ and A. Tursch, 1982. The soft coral community on a sheltered reef quandrant at Laing Island (Papua, New Guinea). Mar. Biol. Vol. 68, 321-332.

Tyree, S., 1992. Tropical coral reef environment rhythmicity and techniques for inducing captive coral spawnings.

V

Van Alstyne, K.L. and V.J. Paul, 1988. The role of secondary metabolites in marine ecology interactions. Proc. 6th Int. Coral reef Symp., Australia. Vol. 1, 175-186.

Veeh, H. H. and K. K. Turekian, 1968.   Cobalt, silver and uranium concentrations of reef building corals in the Pacific Ocean.   Limnol. Oceanogr. 13:304-308.

Von Holt, C. and M. Von Holt, 1968.   Transfer of photosynthetic products from zooxanthellae to coelenterate hosts. Comp. Biochem. Physiol., 27:73-81.

W

Wahbeh, M.I. and A.M. Mahasneh, 1988.   Composition and bacterial utilization of mucus of corals from Aqaba (Red Sea) Jordan.   Proc. 6th Int. Coral reef Symp., Australia.

Wallace, C.C., 1985.   Seasonal peaks and annual fluctuations in recruitment of juvenile scleractinian corals. Mar. Ecol. Prog. Ser. 21:289-298.

Walsh, P. and L. Legendre, 1983.   Photosynthesis of natural phytoplankton under high frequency light conditions simulating those induced by sea surface waves.   Limnol. Oceanogr. 28:688-697.

Watanabe, T., T. Tamiya, A. Oka, M. Hirata and C. Kitajima, 1983.   Improvement of dietary value of live foods for fish larvae by feeding them on omega-3 highly unsaturated fatty acids and fat soluble vitamins.   Bulletin Japanese Society Scientific Fisheries.   49 (3):471-480.

Weber, J.N., 1973.   Incorporation of strontium into reef coral skeletal carbonate.   Geochem. Cosmochim. Acta. 37:2173-2190.

Wilbur, K.M. and K. Simkiss, 1992.   Biomineralization. Academic Press, San Diego, California.

Wilkens, P., 1990.   Invertebrates- Stone and False Corals, Colonial Anemones.   Engelbert Pfriem Verlag, Wuppertal, Germany.

Wilkinson,C.R. and A.C. Cheshire, 1988.   Cross-shelf variations in coral reef structure and function-influence of land and ocean.   Proc. 6th Int. Coral Reef Symp., Australia. 227-233.

—————————————————, D.W. Klumpp and A.D. McKinnion, 1988.   Nutritional spectrum of animals with photosynthetic symbionts-corals and sponges. Proc. 6th Int. Coral Reef Symp., Australia.   Vol. 3, 27-30.

Willis, B.L. and J.K. Oliver, 1988.   Inter-reef dispersal of coral larvae following the annual mass spawning on the Great Barrier Reef.   Proc. 6th Int. Coral reef Symp., Australia.   Vol. 2, 853-859.

Wood, E., 1993.   Reef Corals of the World, Biology and Field Guide.   T.F.H. Publications, Neptune City, N.J.

Worrest, R.C., H. Van Dyke and B. Thomson, 1978. Impact of enhanced simulated solar ultraviolet radiation upon a marine community. Photochemistry and Photobiology, 27:471-478.

Y

Yamazato, K., M. Sato and H. Yamashiro, 1981. Reproductive biology of an alcyonacean coral, Lobophytum crassum (Marenzeller). Proceedings of the 4th International Coral Reef Symposium, Vol. 2, Manila.

Yap, H.T. and E. D. Gomez, 1981. Growth of Acropora pulchra (Brook) in Balinao, Pangasinan, Philippines. Proceedings of the 4th International Coral Reef Symposium, Vol. 2, Manila.

_____, P.M. Alino and E.D. Gomez, 1992. Trends in growth and mortality of three coral species. Mar. Ecol. Prog. Ser. 83:91.

Yonge, C.M., 1963. The biology of coral reefs. Advan. Mar. Biol. 1(4):209.

Yonge, C.M., 1973. The nature of reef building (hermatypic) corals. Bull. Mar. Sci. 23:1.

Young, S.C., 1971. Organic material from scleractinian coral skeletons. I. Variation in composition between several species. Comp. Biochem. Physiol. B 40:113-120.

Z

Zahl, P.A. and J.J. McLaughlin, 1959. Studies in marine biology. IV. On the role of algal cells in the tissues of marine invertebrates. J. Protozool. 6:344-352.

Zann, L., 1988. Marine Community Aquarium - How Fish and Invertebrates Live Together in the Miniature Reef Aquarium. T.F.H. Publications, Neptune City, New Jersey.

Zvalinskii, V.I., V.A. Leletkin, E.A. Titlyanov and M.G. Shaposhnikova, 1980. Photosynthesis and adaptation of corals to irradiance. 2. Oxygen exchange. Photosynthetica, Vol. 14:422-430.

INDEX

ABOUT THE AUTHOR

Dana Riddle has been a marine aquarium hobbyist since 1967. He has had dozens of articles published in leading aquarium journals including Freshwater and Marine Aquarium, Marine Fish Monthly, SeaScope and The Breeder's Registry. Riddle is licensed by the State of Georgia as an environmental specialist. This background has enabled him to objectively study the captive reef. His other interests include photography, art and carpentry. He resides with his wife and daughter in suburban Atlanta, Georgia.